Russian Writers and Society in the Nineteenth Century

Russian Writers and Society in the Nineteenth Century

SECOND, REVISED EDITION

Ronald Hingley

Weidenfeld and Nicolson
London

ISBN 0 297 77375 5

Printed in Great Britain by
Butler & Tanner Ltd, Frome and London

Contents

Maps

Preface to the second edition

This study was originally published in English in 1967, and it has also appeared in Dutch, Finnish, French, German, Italian, Japanese, Spanish and Swedish translation. That it has been widely appreciated, and even received with a measure of affection, is suggested by comments reaching me from all over the world – from non-specialist readers fascinated by Russian culture, as well as from teachers and pupils who know the work as a school and university textbook.

In view of this encouraging response I gladly accepted the publishers' invitation to revise the book. That the process should be more than a mere formality was dictated by the need to re-examine the text in the light of continuing researches into aspects of nineteenth-century Russia. These studies have been reinforced by the discipline of teaching the subject at my university; and also by that of writing books on Russia's Nihilists, Tsars, Political Police and Revolutions as well as a Concise History of the country.

To revise a background study of Russian literature is to be reminded how greatly Russian studies have flourished in the West during the last dozen years. Our understanding of the country has been enhanced by a very spate of scholarly works, and by not a few competent popularising studies as well. The Bibliography has, accordingly, been expanded, being now half as long again as it was in 1967. It does, however, still preserve much of its original character. In particular, the first three sections are, as previously, restricted to works in English, with emphasis on those comparatively general and non-specialist in scope. The result is that many of the most valuable recent contributions have been omitted as over-technical for our particular purposes. This is regrettable, but inevitable – to do full bibliographical justice to a subject so rich would have been impossible owing to considerations of space.

The 'Preface', as it appeared in 1967, has been restyled 'Introduction' and extensively rewritten. So too has the body of the text, which has been purged of not a few inaccuracies, stylistic infelicities and misleading emphases. The aim has been to bring the book into line with my present thinking and way of writing; but again without sacrificing the work's original character. I have also tried to reflect the progress of Russian studies, and of my own understanding of them, by expanding here and curtailing there.

I hope that these labours will continue to be found useful by those who turn to Russia's greatest writers for entertainment or instruction or both.

The transliteration and handling of Russian names are as laid down on pp. xi–xvi of vol. iii of *The Oxford Chekhov* (London, 1964), edited by myself. Dates relating to Russia before 1918 are 'old style': they lag behind the western European calendar by twelve days in the nineteenth century and by thirteen days in the twentieth. References in the text normally give the author's surname only, and for fuller details readers should consult the Bibliography, where authors are listed alphabetically within each of the four sections. Translations into English occurring in the text are my own except where otherwise attributed, and mentions of Tolstoy refer to the novelist Leo Tolstoy except where otherwise indicated.

Some difficulty has occurred in choosing English tenses to describe the many features of imperial Russia which have continued virtually unchanged in Soviet Russia – the climate, for instance, and the ritual of the Orthodox Church. When such topics are discussed in the past tense, this is not necessarily intended to imply that the situation has changed, but is simply a stylistic convenience. An attempt to use tenses strictly would have led to endless qualifications and reservations without corresponding gain.

Warmest thanks are due to five colleagues, past and present: to Professor S.V. Utechin, who kindly read the draft manuscript and whose advice and help are keenly appreciated; to Professor Zbyněk Zeman, with whom I discussed the original conception of the book in the early 1960s, and who introduced me to the publishers; to Mr J.S.G. Simmons for his most valuable advice on Bibliography; to Dr A.J. Krailsheimer; to Dr George Katkov; also to my wife for her constant help and encouragement; and to the Oxford University Press for permitting me to reprint material on pp. 118–19 and 130 from my translations of Chekhov in *The Oxford Chekhov*, vol. viii (London, 1965).

Frilford,   Ronald Hingley
ABINGDON
1977

Introduction

Nineteenth-century Russian literature can delight and inspire even those readers who are totally ignorant of its background, as only pedants would deny. The great Russian writers may, however, be read with even fuller appreciation, and with vastly enhanced understanding, by those who possess some knowledge of the social context. This the present study attempts to supply for the period 1825–1904. It concentrates on prose fiction, the country's supreme cultural achievement, but it does not ignore other literary genres–poetry, drama, criticism, memoir-writing, autobiography – in which nineteenth-century Russians also excelled.

Some readers may feel that the case for such a background study is by no means apparent. Russian fiction does, after all, often seem to explore the human condition in general while remaining remarkably unconcerned with specific individuals in definite places on exact dates. By so frequently generating vagueness and blurred outlines – by identifying their settings as 'a certain provincial centre', 'our town', 'T——District' and the like – the authors almost seem to flaunt a pervasive dislike of precise contexts.

Yet nineteenth-century Russian writers were at work in a specific society, diverse and active, at a lively and eventful period in their country's history. Nor were they as desk-bound as the untutored reader might assume. Pushkin defied the displeasure of his Emperor and Turkish bullets when he attached himself to the Russian army in the field, as described in his *Journey to Erzerum* (1836). Even the sedentary Goncharov travelled round the world, as he recounts in his *Frigate Pallas* (1856). Admittedly one can read the same author's most celebrated work – the novel *Oblomov* – in blissful ignorance of the fact that its publication, in 1859, coincided with the surrender of the great Caucasian guerrilla chief Shamil to the Russians in the mountain village of Gunib. Nor, surely, need we bear in mind, when reading the same novel, that its appearance also coincided with the annexation of large tracts of Chinese territory in the furthest east by the Russian governor-general of Siberia. And yet the century's literary achievements as a whole gain a little in resonance if even circumstances as remote as these are not entirely forgotten. As for the emancipation of the serfs, which took place shortly afterwards in 1861, who can possibly savour the nuances of mid-century Russian writings without some feel for that momentous event? Turgenev's novels and *Sportsman's Sketches* richly illuminate it, yet are themselves no little illumined for those who approach them the other way round – with some previous knowledge of the background.

Foreign involvements are important, and so too are such elemental upheavals as the liberation of fifty million slaves and the later assassination of the Emperor who liberated them. But it is not on such topics alone, or even principally, that the modern reader of the Russian classics stands in need of enlightenment. He also needs to feel the pulsations of everyday life and humble domestic concerns.

How was the Empire administered – not only at the highest level, but also in the most benighted village of Pskov or Tambov Province? What is a zemstvo and what objects were to be found in a peasant's hut? Who wore uniform? Who attended what schools and universities? Who could expect to be 'sent to Siberia', and what might such a fate imply? How did Russians traverse their enormous distances? What was the status of a Cossack, a Jew, a Tatar, a Baltic baron? By what methods – macabre or idiotic, futile or formidable – did the government's internal enemies assault the embattled might of the imperial state? Russian literature and its review of the human tragi-comedy would certainly gain if foreign readers had more precise information on these and many other matters than they often possess.

The present study attempts to answer such questions systematically, and thus to supply readers of a later age and of other nationalities with a background such as Russian nineteenth-century authors took for granted. Many of them wrote with only contemporary compatriots in mind, and would have been astonished at the world's enthusiasm for their work since their death. Some deprecated the very idea of their literature being read abroad – how *could* any foreigner make sense of Russia? 'It will be a long time', Dostoyevsky once warned, 'before people read our writers in Europe, and when they do read them it will be a long time before they understand and appreciate them' (*Diary of a Writer*, July–August 1877). Chekhov said that his *Cherry Orchard* would be a failure in Berlin and Vienna, 'because they have no Lopakhins or students à *la* Trofimov' (letter of 4 March 1904). Our aim has therefore been to supply what Russian writers often leave out. 'Lopakhins' and 'students à *la* Trofimov' are, indeed, precisely the kind of topic on which information is given in this book.

An attempt has also been made to evoke the fascinating atmosphere of imperial Russia. A foreign scholar would be foolish if he sought to rival the vivid pictures of imperial society painted by Pushkin, Herzen, Tolstoy, Turgenev and so many others. But he can draw on their works for illustration, as has been done here. To a limited extent, therefore, this study supplies a commentary on literary works of the period, but it does not even attempt a systematic review of the rich subject-matter of nineteenth-century Russian literature. Illustrations are mainly taken from the better-known works and authors, the temptation to unearth little-known curiosities having been resisted for reasons of space.

The intention is to describe and evoke imperial Russia, not to judge or criticise it – still less to abuse it in tirades similar to those launched against the 'Tsarist régime' (a phrase which will not be found in the text below) by the government which has succeeded it. Cruelty, injustice and exploitation have unhappily been a feature of both pre-1917 and post-1917 Russia, and it is arguable that the similarities between the two outweigh the much-advertised differences. Imperial Russia does have certain attractive features, in that its spokesmen were more modest – less prone than are their successors to claim Russian society of their day as an ideal popular democracy. Imperial Russians were also less apt to obtrude their political system as a model which the rest of the world should be bullied or cajoled into copying – they tended, indeed, to behave as if they were somewhat ashamed of it. But the advantages are by no means all on one side.

Though a comparative evaluation of imperial and Soviet Russia is no concern of the present study, there is a reason why the topic is mentioned here. It is this: that to describe the seamier side of imperial Russia without some qualification is to risk associating oneself by implication with Soviet Russian denunciations of the bad

old days. It therefore seems important to stress once more that a
comparison between the two societies, admittedly an important
topic meriting patient and scholarly consideration, happens not to
be a theme of the present study – though occasional parallels are
drawn in passing. Old Russia and new Russia are both fascinating
subjects, but it is tempting to add that no 'western' person in his
senses would ever have chosen to be a citizen of either. In any case,
as stated, the aim has been to describe, not to judge.

Part One
THE WRITER'S SITUATION

1 Russian literature from 1825 to 1904

Russian writers were producing original work long before 1825, but without creating any of the world's acknowledged literary masterpieces, and though some eight centuries of earlier development provide rewarding material for the literary scholar, he will look in vain for a Russian Dante, Cervantes, Shakespeare, Molière or Goethe. It was only in the 1820s and with the arrival of Pushkin that Russian literature first began to take its place as an important part of European culture.

By 1825 Pushkin was in his middle twenties and well established as a poet. 1825 is also the year in which Chapter One of his novel in verse *Eugene Onegin*, the first important Russian novel as well as one of the greatest, was first published as a whole. The same year witnessed the accession of Nicholas I, together with his suppression of the Decembrist revolt, and is therefore a historical landmark too.

The year 1904, that of Chekhov's death, provides a neat finish to the period. As a master of prose fiction and dramatist, Chekhov was one of the titans, and no Russian writer of comparable status has arisen since. Conveniently for literary historians, his death occurred on the eve of another turning-point in Russian history, the revolution of 1905. Thus the great age of Russian literature ended as it had begun, with an attempt to overthrow the autocracy. Russian literature did not die with Chekhov any more than it had been born with Pushkin, but Chekhov was the last in the line of the Russian classics which had begun with Pushkin and continued through Lermontov, Turgenev, Goncharov, Dostoyevsky and Tolstoy.

THE AGE OF THE NOVEL   Within the eighty years 1825–1904 a core of two and a half decades forms the peak period for the Russian novel, starting with Turgenev's *Rudin* (1856) and ending with Dostoyevsky's *The Brothers Karamazov* (1879–80). This bracket

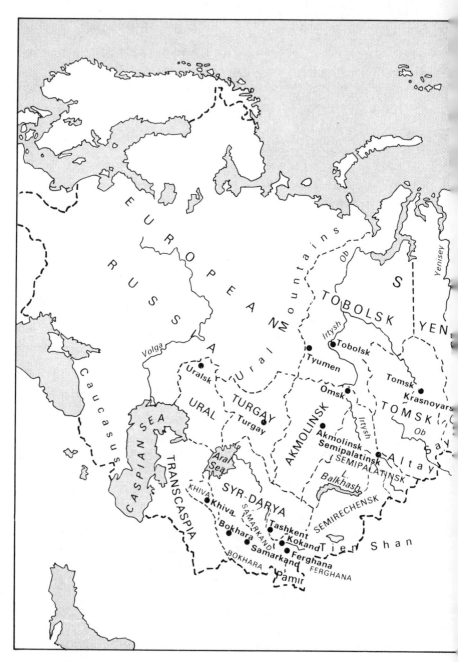

1 *Imperial Russia in the Nineteenth Century*: from the western frontier to the River Yenisey in Central Siberia the greater part of the Empire consisted of a vast plain. To the south and east the frontiers almost everywhere coincided with mountains, rivers or seas.

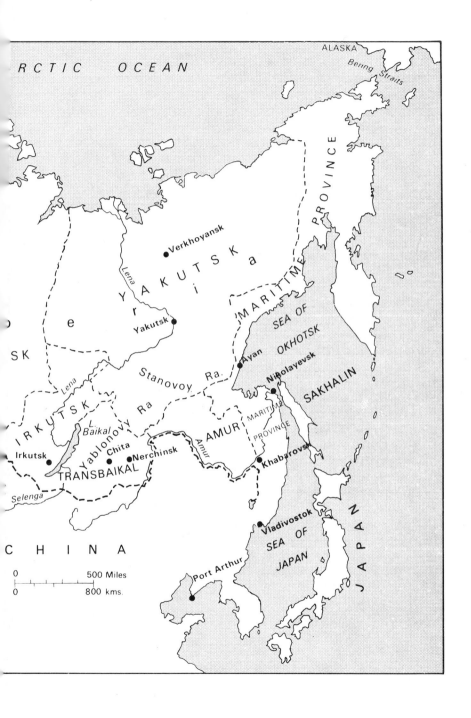

ALASKA

RCTIC OCEAN

Bering Straits

PROVINCE

Verkhoyansk

Y A K U T S K   a

Y   r   i

Lena

MARITIME

Yakutsk

SEA OF
OKHOTSK

Stanovoy   Ra.

Ayan

Nikolayevsk

SAKHALIN

Lena

IRKUTSK

L.
Baikal

Yablonovy   Ra

AMUR

MARITIME
PROVINCE

Irkutsk

Chita

Nerchinsk

Amur

Khabarovsk

TRANSBAIKAL

Selenga

Vladivostok

SEA OF

JAPAN

C H I N A

JAPAN

| 0 | | | 500 Miles |
| 0 | | | 800 kms. |

Port Arthur

includes Tolstoy's two most important novels (*War and Peace* and *Anna Karenin*) and Dostoyevsky's four masterpieces (*Crime and Punishment*; *The Idiot*; *Devils* – also known in translation as *The Possessed* – and *The Brothers Karamazov*). It also includes Goncharov's *Oblomov* and all six of Turgenev's novels (*Rudin*, followed by *A Nest of Gentlefolk*; *On the Eve*; *Fathers and Children*; *Smoke*; *Virgin Soil*). Turgenev's six novels are a formidable body of work taken as a whole, even though some are weaker than others and their total length is considerably less than that of *War and Peace*.

Thus the great age of the novel coincides with the reign of a single Tsar, Alexander II, from 1855 to 1881 – once more as if literature and history had conspired to make a tidy pattern. Many other novels came out in Alexander II's reign as well as those mentioned above. They include Pisemsky's *A Thousand Souls*, Goncharov's *Precipice*, Leskov's *Cathedral Folk* and Saltykov-Shchedrin's *Golovlyov Family*. But none of these can challenge comparison with the thirteen titles listed above. Nor, probably, can any novel written after Alexander II's reign. Tolstoy's *Resurrection* (1899), Sologub's *Little Devil* (1907), Bely's *Petersburg* (1913), Sholokhov's *Quiet Don* (1928–40), Pasternak's *Doctor Zhivago* (1958) and Solzhenitsyn's *The First Circle* (1968) are all remarkable works, while *Foma Gordeyev* (1899), *The Artamonovs' Business* (1925) and others of Gorky's novels have their admirers. But rightly or wrongly none of these works enjoys the distinction of the thirteen titles mentioned in the previous paragraph.

These thirteen titles meet more severe competition from three especially important earlier works which bring the total of leading Russian novels to sixteen. These are Pushkin's *Eugene Onegin* (1825–31), Lermontov's *Hero of Our Time* (1839–40) and Gogol's *Dead Souls*, Part One (1842). All of them have claims to be considered the greatest Russian novel, and all influenced later writing. As these pioneer works suggest, the Russian novel sprang in a sense out of poetry, for the three authors include the greatest Russian poet in Pushkin and another leading poet in Lermontov. Gogol was not a poet, such verse as he wrote being ephemeral, but it may be mentioned that novels were commonly called poems at the time, and *Dead Souls* is so described on its title page.

REALIST FICTION   Literatures often blossom in verse before they flower in prose, and Russian literature was no exception. The 1820s were the golden age of Russian poetry, that of Pushkin and his contemporaries, while the 1830s were the heyday of romantic poetry as represented by Lermontov and Tyutchev (though Tyutchev continued to write until the 1870s). But it was not until the 1840s that an important movement – as opposed to important individual authors – could be discerned in Russian prose.

So keenly did Vissarion Belinsky, who remains the foremost name in Russian criticism, anticipate a great period in his country's literature that he was proclaiming its arrival while it was still little more than a distant potentiality. He used the term 'natural school' to describe what seemed to him the most significant current in Russian prose writing of the 1840s. Prose literature of the time seemed to be evolving under Gogol's influence, which in the end proved less potent than was expected. After sensing the first stirrings of the coming great age of Russian prose, Belinsky died in 1848, too early to see his natural school evolve away from Gogol into Russian realism.

'Realism' and 'realist', used as descriptive terms, are arguably misleading if applied to the dominant strain among Russian writings of the second half of the nineteenth century. But since these terms acquired currency and respectability long ago, it is too late to debate the point in detail. 'Realism' will be used here mainly as a label, and it is hoped that it will be regarded more as the brand name on a varied array of bottles than as a description of contents.

The Russian realist school may be regarded as beginning in the late 1840s. The years 1846–7 show an explosion of talent, less in the quality of work produced than in the number of new writers who then published their first immature work and later achieved fame with more lasting contributions. It was in these years that three leading realist novelists mentioned above made their début: Dostoyevsky with his short novels *Poor Folk* and *The Double* (both 1846), Turgenev with *Khor and Kalinych* (1847) – the first of his *Sportsman's Sketches*, published as a whole in 1852 – and Goncharov with his novel *A Common Story* (1847). Though Tolstoy became known somewhat later (readers had to wait until 1852 for his first publication, *Childhood*), other important realists also brought out their first work in the late 1840s, including Ostrovsky with scenes from his play *All in the Family* (1847). D.V. Grigorovich began publishing in 1844 and brought out *The Village* and *Poor Anton* in 1846 and 1847 – influential stories depicting the miseries of

peasant life. Pisemsky's first published work also belongs to this
period, as does that of Herzen, including his novel *Whose Fault?*
(1845–6). And it was in 1846 that Nekrasov bought the review *The
Contemporary* (St Petersburg, 1836–66), which became for twenty
years the most influential Russian literary monthly and the main
vehicle for the emerging realist movement.

Launched in the late 1840s, Russian realism was producing major
masterpieces ten years later. Of these the thirteen novels from *Rudin*
to *The Brothers Karamazov*, mentioned above, represent the
supreme achievement, but form only a small part of the total corpus.
To them may be added many minor works by the four novelists
concerned (Turgenev, Tolstoy, Dostoyevsky and Goncharov) as
well as the writings of Pisemsky, Leskov, S.T. Aksakov, Ostrovsky
and others.

Though realism has been deprecated as a descriptive term, being
used more as a label, certain characteristics do loosely unite the Russian writers to whom the term is commonly applied. These include
a preference for portraying Russian life contemporary with the
author in a Russian setting; a straightforward, plain, functional
style; a tendency to include detailed factual description of such
things as landscape, dress and physical appearance.

Not all works termed realist fully conform with these qualifications. Thus *War and Peace* does not portray contemporary Russian
life, being a historical novel set more than half a century before the
period in which it was written. Aksakov's *Family Chronicle* (1856)
and *The Childhood of Bagrov the Grandson* (1858) are also set in
the past, and draw, like *War and Peace*, on the author's own family
history. Turgenev's *Smoke* does not take place in Russia, but in
Baden-Baden. Then again, no one could call the style of Dostoyevsky's earliest fiction plain, modelled as it is on that of the exu-
berantly tortuous Gogol. Nor is detailed factual description by any
means always the rule. Tolstoy's later 'popular' stories convey
simple morals to simple people in spare language, while Chekhov's
descriptions are so economical that they make some of his prede-
cessors seem lush by comparison. Generally speaking, however, the
characteristics given above are valid for the Russian realists.

Others which are sometimes advanced apply less fully. When
critics claim neglect of plot in favour of characterisation as a feature
of the school, one wonders whether they are misled by the leisurely
pace of some Russian realists. A plot may be slow-moving, as in

Goncharov's *Oblomov*, yet effective. Some realist works – *Crime and Punishment* and *Anna Karenin* – are triumphs of plot construction, and even Chekhov's stories often have more plot than is sometimes conceded to them. Another quality claimed for the realist school is human sympathy. 'People are not good or bad, they are only more or less unhappy and deserving of sympathy – this may be taken as the formula of all the Russian novelists from Turgenev to Chekhov' (Mirsky, pp. 170–1). True, Goncharov, Turgenev and Tolstoy do bear out this claim. But what of Dostoyevsky's monumental villains? What of Saltykov-Shchedrin's monstrous *Golovlyov Family*? Or of the ogres of insensitivity and selfishness in the work of Chekhov?

Are these works realist in being 'true to life', to mention a cliché which often comes up in such discussions? It is not always clear just what those who use the phrase understand by 'life', which can mean different things to different people, as the evidence of literature confirms. One of the attractions of literature, in fact, is that each author recreates life according to his personal vision of it. And even if 'truth to life' could be accepted as a criterion, it would apply only partially to the Russian realists. Gogol himself has sometimes been claimed as a realist and even as the father of Russian realism, a view difficult to sustain. But Gogol was a caricaturist and dealt in exaggeration. That a man should wake up one day to find his nose missing and should later notice it going about disguised as a senior civil servant – this typical episode from his story *The Nose* (1835) is hardly true to the average man's experience of life. Nor have most average men had private interviews with the devil, as happens to one of Dostoyevsky's heroes, Ivan Karamazov. Nor yet, even in nineteenth-century Russia, have prostitutes, epileptics, suicides, murderers, lunatics and torturers been as prevalent as Dostoyevsky's works suggest. Is Turgenev's treatment of love realist? Or is it, at least in the vulgar sense of the word, romantic? Even Chekhov, apparently truest to life of all, is suspect. Surely relationships between men and women are not so uniformly frustrating as is indicated in his pages – any more than they are always as sentimental and Wertheresque as Turgenev tends to imply.

Perhaps the most important quality of the great Russian realists, and one which more than any other unites them, is a certain common attitude to themselves and their world – an agreement on the importance of being, in the best sense of the word, earnest. They were

serious about man and man's destiny in a new and characteristically
Russian way. Some held strong views and were determined to
propagate them, while others were less dogmatic, but sought at least
to formulate the riddles of Russian life and human existence even
if they could not solve them. This seriousness is surely one of the
reasons why Russian nineteenth-century literature has caught the
imagination of the world – especially as some writers, including
Gogol, Dostoyevsky and Chekhov, combine it with humour simul-
taneously grotesque and subtle. Humorous or not, the Russian
realist author usually felt himself to be more than a mere entertainer.

The Russian novel lost impetus at the end of the 1870s. The year
1881, that of Alexander II's assassination, was also that of Dostoyevsky's death. Turgenev died two years later, and Tolstoy, who
was to live on until 1910, died a sort of literary death in the late
seventies at the time of his conversion to his own brand of Christianity. He was never to repeat the triumph of *Anna Karenin* and
almost turned his back on fiction as he had hitherto practised it in
order to become a moralist. Goncharov too was a spent force long
before his death in 1891.

CHEKHOV AND THE DRAMA   Thus the age of the giants was over
by 1880, when Chekhov published his first writings. During the
next twenty-five years he stood well above all other still-living
Russian writers of prose fiction except for Tolstoy, now in semi-
retirement as a novelist. Chekhov himself was never a novelist, since
his only essay in the genre – *The Shooting Party* (1884) – is a light-
weight effort. He began his literary career as the writer of facetious
sketches about comic mothers-in-law and the like, but had found
his level by 1888 as an original short-story writer. The three score
of stories written between the beginning of that year and his death
give him a special position in Russian literature, and the importance
of this corpus is arguably even greater than that of *War and Peace*
or *The Brothers Karamazov*. No other Russian except Gogol, Tolstoy and Leskov, whose methods were different, is worth mention-
ing in the same breath as a short-story writer.

Chekhov also became Russia's greatest dramatist, though on his
home territory Ostrovsky with his larger dramatic *œuvre* is a more
serious rival than he seems to foreigners. Otherwise Russian drama
of the period can most simply be regarded as a series of brilliant
individual efforts by authors who have all written other dramatic

work, but are remembered by most theatre-goers for one play only: Griboyedov for *Woe from Wit* (written 1822–4); Gogol for *The Inspector General* (1836); Turgenev for *A Month in the Country* (1850); Tolstoy for *The Power of Darkness* (1888) and Gorky for *The Lower Depths* (1902).

MEMOIRS A few examples of autobiographies and collections of memoirs must also be mentioned, among which Herzen's *My Past and Thoughts* (1852–68) is outstanding. It is often used below to illustrate aspects of Nicholas I's Russia, and its value is enhanced by the fact that it was not subject to Russian censorship, having been produced abroad. Gorky's story of his early life, often considered his most important work, covers the period considered here, though it was written and published later, in three parts: *Childhood* (1913–14); *In the World* (1915–16) and *My Universities* (1923). To this must be added the same author's much overrated *Reminiscences* (1924–31) of writers who include Chekhov and Tolstoy.

Thinly disguised autobiographies or family reminiscences – written to a great extent about the author himself and his own family, but preserving the outward form of fiction – also occupy an honoured place in nineteenth-century Russian literature. The genre includes Aksakov's reminiscences and studies of family history going back into the eighteenth century, of which his *Family Chronicle* and *Childhood of Bagrov the Grandson* were mentioned above. It also includes Dostoyevsky's *Memoirs from the House of the Dead* (1862); and Tolstoy's trilogy, *Childhood* (1852), *Boyhood* (1854) and *Youth* (1857). These works all provide valuable evidence on the authors themselves in specific Russian social contexts, even if the main characters bear the names 'Bagrov', 'Goryanchikov' and 'Irtenyev' rather than their real names – Aksakov, Dostoyevsky and Tolstoy respectively.

POETRY This brief sketch of Russian literature of the great age must be ended with some further reference to poetry. After the blossoming of Pushkin, Lermontov and other poets of the 1820s and 1830s, verse yielded first place to prose until the end of the century, but by no means disappeared from the scene. In mid-century it was sustained by Nekrasov's writings, often propagandist in intent, but original and memorable, his longest and most important work being *Who Can Be Happy in Russia?* (1873–6). Nekrasov proclaimed himself obsessed with his duties as a citizen to lighten the lot of his fellow-Russians, especially the downtrodden peasantry. Among other mid-century poets Tyutchev, who continued to write, Afanasy Fet and Apollon Maykov, were less civic-minded than Nekrasov and more concerned to create works of art. At the turn of the century the desire to rise above Russian writers' traditional preoccupations with their civic duty contributed to the philosophy of the symbolist movement in Russian poetry, of which Blok was the most prominent representative.

2 *The writer's life and mission*

SOCIAL POSITION Many Russian nineteenth-century writers belonged, particularly in the first part of the period, to the Russian gentry, that is to the most privileged class. Some of the most important, moreover – notably Pushkin, Turgenev and Tolstoy – sprang from an élite within the gentry, that of substantial country landowners. Such families had been supported for generations by serf labour, an influence illustrated as potentially demoralising by one who was not a member of the group, but of merchant extraction – Goncharov – in the novel *Oblomov*.

Membership of the gentry was not necessarily a sign of exalted social origin. Dostoyevsky too belonged to it, but was resentful of such social superiors as Turgenev and Tolstoy. Dostoyevsky's father was an army doctor who had retired from the service to practise as a civilian before his novelist son was born, and who in course of time had decided to add to the status of gentleman, which he possessed in law, the cachet of rural landowner. He accordingly bought two villages complete with over a hundred resident serfs. A few years later he was murdered by these same serfs under circumstances which remain mysterious – an occurrence by no means unique in the annals of Russian county families.

In the course of the century literature and cultural life were increasingly invaded by persons of humble social origin known as *raznochintsy*, of which 'other ranks' is a rough English translation. Belinsky, son of a poor doctor, was one of these, and so too were Chernyshevsky and Dobrolyubov, who belonged to the most characteristic group of the *raznochintsy*, that of the seminarists (pupils of seminaries for the sons of priests). Chekhov was a grocer's son and Gorky, another social upstart, came from a poor family and worked in his youth as a shop-boy, baker and washer-up on a Volga steamship, thus graduating as the first major writer closely associated with the Russian proletariat. From the largest and most humble social class, the peasantry, literature had few recruits.

HAZARDS OF AUTHORSHIP Having considered how certain Russian writers were born, we may also profitably note how some of them died, since this makes it easier to understand a Russian's attitude to his literature. There is a tendency for modern readers to regard writers of the last century as sedentary creatures musing gently at their desks – an impression which seems borne out by the leisurely pace of Russian novels, so often set in the dreamy world of country estates where life flows on uneventfully through several hundred pages. Most nineteenth-century Russian writers were, however, anything but serene, benevolent, typically 'Victorian' men of letters. Nor did Russia, where life and liberty were such precarious commodities, generate the atmosphere of a Trollopian deanery – as readers of Leskov's *Cathedral Folk* can testify.

Two leading poets were killed in duels: Pushkin at the age of thirty-seven and Lermontov at twenty-seven. Both had already been exiled – Pushkin for showing leanings towards atheism in a private letter intercepted by the authorities, Lermontov for blaming Pushkin's death on the imperial Establishment in his *Death of a Poet* (circulated in 1837). Both poets felt persecuted by authority, but Lermontov was at least temperamentally equipped to derive perverse satisfaction from this. Not so Pushkin, who especially resented the authorities' refusal to permit him to travel abroad. After 1826, when he was released from exile, interviewed by Nicholas I and placed under the Tsar's personal protection, he still felt crushed by the weight of imperial patronage, exercised through Nicholas's chief of gendarmes, Count Benckendorff.

Many of Pushkin's contemporaries were punished for their part in the Decembrist revolt of 1825. Several were poets: Kondraty Ryleyev (one of the five leaders who were hanged), Alexander Odoyevsky and Wilhelm Küchelbecker (who were exiled to Siberia). Another writer and friend of Pushkin's, the romantic novelist and poet Alexander Bestuzhev, who wrote under the pseudonym Marlinsky, was sentenced to twenty years' hard labour, later commuted to service in the Caucasus as a private soldier, for his part in the uprising.

A combination of these misfortunes overtook Dostoyevsky. Sentenced in 1849 to execution for his association with a political discussion group, he was led out with a number of others to be shot – a sadistic joke staged on the direct orders of Nicholas I. After some of the victims had been clothed in shrouds by soldiers, an especially grim detail, commutation of the sentence was – by previous arrangement – announced at the last possible moment. Dostoyevsky was compelled to spend some ten years in Siberia, four as a convict in the gaol at Omsk, and the rest as a private and officer in a Siberian army unit, followed by a period of exile as a civilian.

Dostoyevsky had, perhaps, deliberately courted disaster. But even Turgenev, altogether more cautious, did not escape criminal proceedings. His punishment was milder, since he was only kept under arrest for a month in 1852 and then exiled to his country estate for sixteen months. The reason for this is typical of the country: he had indiscreetly written an obituary of Gogol, published in Moscow at a time when articles on Gogol were prohibited in the St Petersburg press. As this reminds one, the authorities commonly reacted to a leading writer's death with nervousness and precautionary measures, since it was traditional for these obsequies to be celebrated with political demonstrations. When, in due course, Turgenev himself died over thirty years later the same tradition still flourished (see p. 102). He would, incidentally, have perished far earlier if Tolstoy had had his way. A bitter quarrel between the two writers came to a head in 1861, when Turgenev insulted Tolstoy, who challenged him to a duel on most unusual terms, since it was to be fought with rifles and even without seconds. Fortunately this unhappy event did not take place, as the world might otherwise have been robbed of *Smoke*, *Virgin Soil*, *War and Peace*, *Anna Karenin* and much else.

The tally of distinguished exiles was large. Besides some already mentioned, Herzen was banished to Perm, Vyatka (now Kirov), Vladimir and Novgorod at various times before leaving Russia for ever in 1847. The radical critic and political thinker Chernyshevsky is one among many literary figures who suffered more severely. He spent over half his adult life in prison and exile, mainly in remote parts of Siberia, and his resolute defiance of authority makes him one of the most illustrious political prisoners. The short-story writer Korolenko was exiled to Siberia (from 1879 to 1885) and was not permitted to live in St Petersburg until 1895. Many other writers also met violent or sudden fates in addition to the casualties from duels mentioned above. The playwright-diplomat Griboyedov was torn to pieces by a Persian mob in 1829; the radical publicist Pisarev drowned in 1868; the short-story writer Garshin committed suicide by jumping down the well of a staircase in 1888. Others became deranged (Gogol, Goncharov), or were officially declared so in defiance of the facts (Chaadayev).

There were, however, authors who contrived to die from natural causes, not directly assisted by authority. Tuberculosis, that great nineteenth-century scourge, claimed two important victims: Belinsky at the age of thirty-six and Chekhov at the age of forty-four. But the rugged Tolstoy survived until his ninth decade. Like Pasternak later, he was protected by international fame from the persecution which he seemed to challenge, and suffered only the – to him – ludicrous fate of being excommunicated by the Russian Orthodox Church in 1901, on which occasion he 'positively refused to accept congratulations'. But even Tolstoy presumably hastened his end by running away from home at the age of eighty-two.

WRITING FOR A LIVING   Though nineteenth-century Russian imaginative writings may suggest that their authors were exclusively concerned with the general human condition and with problems of philosophy, religion or ethics, their private correspondence tends to reveal an obsession with the more mundane topic of money. They lived in the everyday world as well as in the world of the imagination, and there were times when most of them were aware that they and their families needed to be fed and housed. Their general level of financial competence was not, however, high.

The main nineteenth-century Russian writers were all professional authors, depending at least in part on the earnings of their pens. Even Pushkin, very much a member of the élite, could point the contrast with an earlier age when he said, 'I am not one of our eighteenth-century writers', and explained that, though he wrote for himself, he published for money (letter of 8 March 1824). He also said that he looked on his finished poems 'as a cobbler looks on a pair of boots. I sell for profit' (letter of March 1823). Prevented by the Tsar from publishing *Boris Godunov* (written in 1825), Pushkin told Benckendorff that for him to be deprived of some 15,000 roubles which his tragedy might bring him would be an 'inconvenience' (letter of 7 January 1830). This was a masterly understatement, since Pushkin was in fact extremely angry.

Other heirs to substantial properties, Tolstoy and Turgenev, were also eager to earn money from their writings. True, Tolstoy antagonised his wife in 1891 by renouncing the copyright of all his works written after *Anna Karenin*, and thus ceased to receive royalties. He had in effect taken a vow of poverty, but Countess Tolstoy most certainly had not, and retained control over his earlier copyrights. The family could afford the luxury of such manœuvres, but Tolstoy had behaved more conventionally as a young man. His short novel *Cossacks* (1863) might never have been published at all, had he not lost a large sum of money at cards and been compelled to accept an advance for the work from the publisher of the monthly *Russian Herald*, M.N. Katkov.

Such episodes were the very fabric of Dostoyevsky's life. He was occasionally forced to pawn his trousers and underclothes, and was for many years a compulsive gambler. Few authors have signed a literary contract more disadvantageous than that for the short novel *The Gambler*, which bound him to the rapacious publisher Stellovsky. This agreement contained penalty clauses stopping just short of hard labour for life. Yet the affair had a happy ending: Dostoyevsky hurriedly engaged a stenographer, completed a minor masterpiece with lightning rapidity, fulfilled his contract and married his amanuensis – excellent results for a few weeks' work.

Chekhov always wrote for money after becoming the chief provider for a large family in his early twenties. As a young man he often had difficulty in extracting his fees from editors, who would try to fob him off with payment in kind. One indulgently told him to 'see my tailor and order yourself some trousers'. Or theatre tickets might be offered in place of cash. In 1899 Chekhov, by now a long-established writer, sold the copyright of all his published work except drama to the publisher A.F. Marks by a contract which turned out spectacularly unprofitable to the author. In common with most Russian nineteenth-century authors he needed a competent literary agent, but that honourable profession was not, alas, practised in nineteenth-century Russia.

As cannot be too strongly stressed, the biographies, correspondence and private observations of Russian nineteenth-century authors contain infinitely more references to hard cash than to ultimate profundities. Harassed by financial worries, writers were nevertheless casual in their financial arrangements. Loans were readily granted, gambled away or forgotten by the debtor. Frenzied appeals, orgies of self-justification, squabbles and reconciliations were the usual accompaniment to these transactions. A famous literary quarrel, that between Turgenev and Dostoyevsky, shows a leading westernist and slavophile locked in conflict over principles, but it is tempting to see the real bone of contention in something less superficial – the fifty thalers lent by Turgenev to Dostoyevsky in 1865. Dostoyevsky had offered to repay the money within three weeks, but failed to do so for ten years. Turgenev might forgive him, but that was not the point – Dostoyevsky could not forgive Turgenev for doing him the favour in the first place.

Where established authors were involved, an advance would often have been paid and spent before serious work had even begun – a custom by no means confined to the writers of Russia. For periodical publication authors were usually paid so many roubles per signature or 'printer's sheet' (equivalent to about sixteen pages of a book) in the case of longer works, and so much a line for shorter items. It would, however, be excessively cynical to ascribe the inordinate length (as is sometimes felt) of the typical Russian novel to this system of payment by bulk. After periodical publication the author was usually free to market his work anew for issue in book form.

Established writers were naturally paid at preferential rates. Dostoyevsky, who became popular comparatively late in life, sometimes expressed envy of Turgenev and Tolstoy, since they regularly commanded many more roubles per printer's sheet than he could obtain. This seemed grossly unfair since his two rivals did not need the money as urgently as a 'literary proletarian' – Dostoyevsky's own description of himself.

SERIALISATION   It was in the periodical press, not in book form, that the bulk of nineteenth-century Russian literature first appeared – as has most Russian and Soviet Russian literature down to the present day. Each of the sixteen leading Russian novels, referred to on p. 101 above, first saw the light of day in a periodical, except for Gogol's *Dead Souls* and – with certain qualifications – Pushkin's *Eugene Onegin* (see Pushkin, *Eugene Onegin*, ed. Nabokov, i, pp. 74–83; for further information on periodicals, see also pp. 157–60 below).

Owing to this procedure nearly all Russian novels were first brought out in serial form, as were those of many leading French and English authors of the period, including Balzac and Dickens.

It was, consequently, by no means uncommon for a large part of a nineteenth-century novel, whether Russian, French or English, to be already in print when the ending was little more than a vague project. Thus Tolstoy's *War and Peace* began to appear in the monthly *Russian Herald* in January and February 1865 under the title *1805*. A second batch entitled *War* came out in the same review in February, March and April 1866. At this stage Tolstoy planned a happy ending. The third and final instalment was to be called *All's Well that Ends Well*, and in it Prince Andrew's life was to be preserved (Christian, pp. 5–7). In this instance, however, the author did not maintain serial publication, for though *War and Peace* continued to roll majestically on, the rest of it was first published in book form.

Dostoyevsky was also accustomed to seeing large batches of his novels in print long before the endings had been written, but was not greatly hampered by one disadvantage of the method – that early chapters of a book published in this way commit an author so that he is no longer free to revise his over-all plan. For someone so apparently disorganised, Dostoyevsky had a surprisingly clear idea of the future development of his unfinished novels, as his published *Notebooks* show. He claimed that he never accepted an advance from a publisher for what he called a blank space: 'When I've received money in advance I have always sold something existing, i.e. I've only sold myself at a point when the poetic idea has already been born and has ripened as far as possible. I have not taken money in advance *for a blank space*, i.e. in the hope of *thinking up* and *composing* a novel by a given date' (Hingley, *The Undiscovered Dostoyevsky*, p. 108).

'COMMITMENT' Few Russian writers were pillars of church and state. They tended to be politically disaffected, with some striking exceptions such as the ultra-monarchist Gogol, and also Dostoyevsky after his return from Siberian exile. But even they were scarcely bulwarks of the imperial system, for all the support which they gave it, each in his own eccentric style. Moreover, Gogol's name became a rallying point for radicals, much to his own surprise and horror. Hence the punishment imposed on Turgenev for his ill-judged obituary of Gogol.

Radicals or reactionaries, Russian writers tended to be politically engaged. Many displayed crusading fervour, and had political, ethical, religious, moral or philosophical lessons to teach. In a country lacking free institutions, literature – hampered though it was by censorship – yet offered some scope for airing political and social opinions. Hence the Russian tradition of looking on the writer as a sage who might perhaps solve the riddle of existence and who was permanently engaged in a 'search for truth', to quote a formula far too commonly invoked when Russians discuss the writer's role.

Many Russian writers considered themselves in direct touch with ultimate truth. An extreme case is Gogol, whose great novel *Dead Souls*, Part One, was planned as the first instalment of a trilogy designed to regenerate Russia. Parts Two and Three were to be increasingly positive, and to supply the purgatorio and paradiso to the inferno of Part One. But Gogol's genius shone with full brilliance only when he described the squalid and absurd. Consequently only a fragment of the edifying Part Two, and none of the designedly still more edifying Part Three, saw the light of day. Unable to portray virtuous characters convincingly in fiction, he proceeded to address the nation with sermons on conduct disguised as letters. This strange document, *Select Passages from a Correspondence with Friends* (1847), so infuriated Belinsky that he denounced Gogol in an open letter as 'prophet of the knout, apostle of ignorance, champion of obscurantism and panegyrist of Tatar manners'. His indignation is understandable since Gogol had gone so far as to recommend the flogging of serfs.

Dostoyevsky's views were in some ways a diluted version of Gogol's, though moderation is not a quality easily associated with Dostoyevsky. His great sequence of journalistic harangues, *The Diary of a Writer* (1873–81), shows him wholeheartedly committed to the instruction of humanity, and occupies a place in his biography comparable to that of the *Select Passages* in Gogol's. In his greatest works of fiction too Dostoyevsky sought to propagate his system of ideas.

Tolstoy was another propagandist and teacher. As is the general human lot, he found this tendency increasing as he became older. Content to develop a comparatively academic philosophy of history in *War and Peace*, he later descended to a more practical level by urging his readers to stop smoking and fornicating. He even discouraged them from reading his own early fiction. He also inspired a movement based on the ethic of practical Christianity and including the principle of non-violence.

Gogol, Dostoyevsky and Tolstoy cannot properly be called seekers for truth, since they believed themselves to have found it. Other writers were less committed to doctrine, but still accepted some degree of social obligation, considering it their function at least to present political and social problems, even if they had no specific solutions to offer.

Turgenev was among those who adopted the spectator's role rather than that of active participant. His novels span Alexander II's reign and illustrate several important issues of the period. *Rudin* presents the 'superfluous man' or odd-man-out, a typical figure in Russian society already described by Pushkin, Lermontov and others; *A Nest of Gentlefolk* shows old-fashioned Russian country life and the pressures of European influence; *On the Eve* examines the 'man of action', a concept which has exercised many other Russian writers too; *Fathers and Children* describes the clash between the idealists of the 1840s and the radicals of the 1860s, while *Smoke* treats the conflict between westernists and slavophiles (see pp. 168–9), and *Virgin Soil* describes the populist movement (see pp. 173–5). Turgenev might accordingly have been designed by nature to provide essay subjects for students of nineteenth-century Russian social history. He himself held political and social views, being a moderate liberal and westernist, an opponent of serfdom and so on, but his approach to social problems was too objective and equable to suit many of his contemporaries.

Chekhov was an outstandingly apolitical writer. As many comments in his letters show, he resented the tradition whereby writers were pestered by critics and busybodies, and in effect ordered to mobilise themselves on behalf of political and social causes. He hated preaching and being preached at, but he too took his role as social observer seriously. He illustrated such problems as the decline of the landowners, the effects of following Tolstoy's teaching in everyday life and the rise of Russian industry. On the abiding problem of the Russian peasant his contributions were superbly eloquent in his characteristically quiet tone. However, neither on this subject nor on any other did Chekhov's role as a social commentator cloud his vision as a creative artist.

There were also many writers and critics who expressed or tried to express extreme left-wing views which they put forward within the narrow – but varying – limits permitted by censorship. Later developments make this school seem the most influential of all. In a sense it has proved the winning side, though the claims of the present-day Communist Party of the Soviet Union to be the direct heir of Herzen and Chernyshevsky should not be accepted uncritically. Among radicals and socialists Herzen and Gorky have produced the outstanding autobiographies mentioned above, but on the whole members of this group did not belong to the front rank of imaginative writers. Nekrasov and Gorky are the leading creative artists among the radicals, the bulk of Gorky's work falling outside the period studied here.

The radical strain was more dominant in criticism than on the creative side. Even in criticism it was far indeed from enjoying a monopoly, but the greatest of all Russian critics, Belinsky, was a radical, as were his successors, Chernyshevsky and Dobrolyubov. One striking feature of much Russian criticism from Belinsky onwards is the tendency to ignore the literary values and methods of a work of art and to quarry literary works for texts to political and social sermons.

Part Two
THE EMPIRE

3 Geography

FRONTIERS   By the end of the nineteenth century the Empire's boundaries enclosed roughly the same huge area as that of its successor state the USSR. The differences were greatest on the western frontiers where Finland and Poland were both part of the territory ruled by the Tsar, but whereas Finland enjoyed a large measure of autonomy, Poland was a subject nation – especially after 1863. From 1815 to the end of the century Russia's western frontiers remained comparatively stable, but in the south and east conditions were fluid, and vast new areas were added to the growing Empire.

Most of the Caucasus, including Transcaucasia, came under Russian rule by submission or conquest between 1801 and 1829. This applies to most of Georgia; to Armenia except for the part which remained to Turkey; and to Azerbaydzhan. Meanwhile the mountaineers of the central Caucasus still resisted in their craggy fortresses, not being completely pacified even with the surrender of their leader Shamil in 1859 and the completed annexation of Circassia in 1864.

The next scene of large-scale expansion was the far east of Siberia. For nearly two centuries the frontier with China had remained as fixed in 1689 by the Treaty of Nerchinsk, but now two new treaties were imposed on the Chinese by N.N. Muravyov, Russian governor-general of Eastern Siberia. By these the Chinese ceded two areas in 1858 and 1860: the left bank of the River Amur and the Maritime Province on the Sea of Japan down to the port of Vladivostok, founded in 1860. The end of the century saw a further important but short-lived strategic gain when the Russians set up their naval base at Port Arthur – acquired on lease from China in 1898, but lost to the Japanese in the Russo-Japanese War of 1904–5. For the fast-expanding Empire to yield up territory, however small, was exceptional, but an earlier, voluntary instance of this had occurred

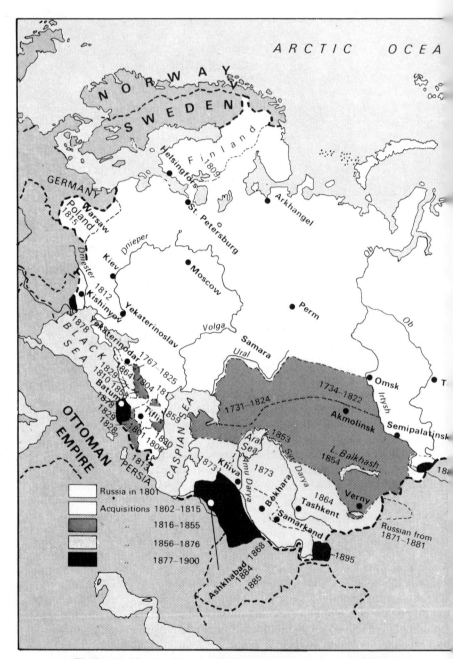

Map labels: ARCTIC OCEAN, NORWAY, SWEDEN, Finland 1809, Helsingfors, GERMANY, Warsaw Poland 1815, Dniester 1812, Kiev, Dnieper, Kishinyev, St. Petersburg, Arkhangel, Moscow, Yekaterinoslav, Perm, Ob, Volga, Ural, Samara, Ekaterinodar, BLACK SEA, 1829, 1804, 1767–1825, 1864, 1878, 1828, Batum, 1878, Tiflis, 1859, OTTOMAN EMPIRE, PERSIA, 1801, 1806, 1830, 1813, CASPIAN SEA, 1734–1822, 1731–1824, Omsk, Irtysh, Semipalatinsk, Akmolinsk, 1853, L. Balkhash 1854, Aral Sea, Amu Darya, Khiva 1873, Syr Darya, Bokhara, Verny, 1864, Tashkent, Samarkand, Russian from 1871–1881, Ashkhabad 1868, 1884, 1885, 1895, T

Legend:
- Russia in 1801
- Acquisitions 1802–1815
- " 1816–1855
- " 1856–1876
- " 1877–1900

2 *The Imperial Russian Frontier:* the Russian Empire at the beginning of the twentieth century, showing the main territorial changes which occurred during, and just before, the period under review. The main areas of expansion in the nineteenth century were: Finland (1809); Poland (1815); the Caucasus (1801–59); the Far East (1858–60); Central Asia (1853–85). The largest area ceded by Russia was Alaska, sold to the United States in 1867.

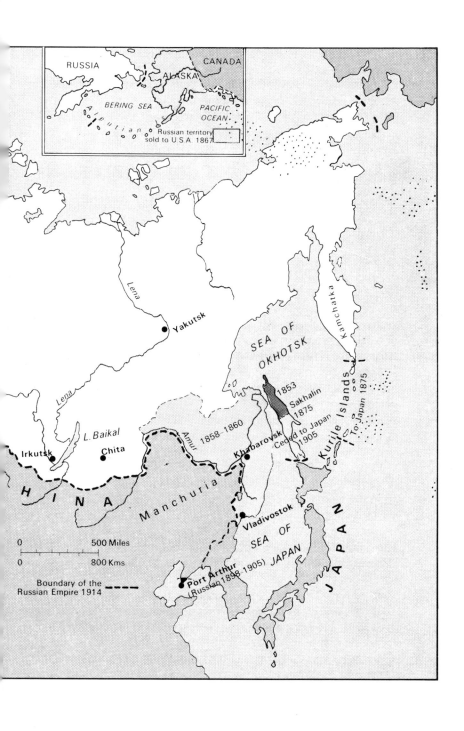

RUSSIA
CANADA
ALASKA
BERING SEA
Aleutian
PACIFIC OCEAN
Russian territory sold to U.S.A. 1867

Lena

Yakutsk

SEA OF
OKHOTSK

Kamchatka

Lena

L. Baikal

Amur

1858-1860

1853

Sakhalin
1875

Ceded to Japan
1905

Kurile Islands

To Japan 1875

Irkutsk

Chita

Khabarovsk

H I N A

Manchuria

Vladivostok

SEA OF
JAPAN

J A P A N

0   500 Miles
0   800 Kms.

Boundary of the
Russian Empire 1914

Port Arthur
(Russian 1898-1905)

in 1867 when Russia sold Alaska to the United States for eight
million dollars.

Central Asia followed the Far East as the chief arena of expansion,
often at the initiative of empire-building Russian military governors
in the locality, and in retaliation against raids by those whom the
Russians considered marauding nomads. In 1868 the Emir of Bokhara was forced to yield part of his kingdom, including Samarkand,
while accepting Russian protection and dependent status. He was
followed by the Khan of Khiva in 1873. In 1876 the Khanate of
Kokand was subdued, and fear of Russian designs on India led the
British to look to the defences of the Khyber Pass. By 1885 Russia
had also annexed the whole of Transcaspia.

By its very size imperial Russia seemed to threaten western
Europe. With some eight and a half million square miles of territory,
of which about one quarter was in Europe and the remainder in Asia,
it was larger than the entire North American continent. At one time
the British Empire covered an even vaster expanse, but that was
scattered over the globe. There was nowhere a continuous stretch
of territory, ruled from a single centre, of comparable size to the
Russian Empire. Siberia above all caught the world's imagination
as dwarfing even European Russia. With its vast coniferous forests,
huge rivers, extreme winter climate, extensive mountain ranges and
general unsavoury repute, Russia in Asia seemed like another
planet. Its area, one and a half times that of Europe, was calculated
as greater than that of the face of the full moon.

RELIEF   European Russia and much of Siberia together form a
huge plain flanked by mountains to east and south and extending
from the western frontier through sixty degrees of longitude to the
River Yenisey in central Siberia. The Ural Mountains (highest
point 6,210 feet), the boundary between Russia in Europe and
Russia in Asia, form a natural barrier, but one easily traversed. In
the west the Valday Upland, rising to little more than 1,000 feet
south-east of St Petersburg, and the Central Russian Upland, to
the south of Moscow, form even less of an obstacle. It is on the
Empire's southern and eastern marches that major natural barriers
are found. They begin in the south-west with the Carpathian Mountains and Crimean Upland, continuing in grander style with the
Caucasian chain and – beyond the Caspian – the Pamir, Tien-Shan,
Altay and Sayan ranges. Eastern Siberia is crossed by mountain

chains, the Yablonovy, Stanovoy and others. Accordingly the Empire's southern border was almost everywhere fenced off by mountains or seas.

HYDROGRAPHY   Russia has the two largest lakes in the world, so large that they are termed seas: the Caspian and the Aral. She also has the largest lakes in Asia (Baikal and Balkhash) and in Europe (Ladoga and Onega).

The country is well stocked with rivers, having the longest in Europe, the Volga (2,300 miles in length), and three Siberian rivers which dwarf even the Volga: the Ob (3,500 miles from the source of its chief tributary, the Irtysh), the Yenisey (3,700 miles from the source of the Selenga) and the Lena (2,670 miles).

Many important rivers of European Russia rise in a small area of the western midlands formed by the Valday and Central Russian Uplands. They include the Volga and its tributary the Oka, and also the Western Dvina, Dnieper and Don. Being close to each other and easily linked by portages in early times – and later by canal – the rivers provided a valuable communication network, especially as most are slow-flowing and navigable far upstream. But many become icebound in winter, flood heavily in spring and form shallows in summer. Another disadvantage: the rivers do not seem, ultimately to lead anywhere, but pour into landlocked or partly landlocked seas: the Caspian, the Sea of Azov, the Black Sea, the Gulf of Riga, the Gulf of Finland and the White Sea. Others, including the three longest Siberian rivers, drain into the inhospitable Arctic Ocean. As for ports, many of these too become icebound for long periods, a factor further restricting access to the world's sea routes.

VEGETATION   Russia consists of uneven, broad vegetational zones running in roughly horizontal bands across European Russia and Siberia. In the extreme north are the Arctic wastes and tundra, thinly populated and of slight historical importance. South of those are the two most important vegetational zones: first the forest and then, to the south of that, the steppe – the word denotes a large treeless plain or prairie covered with herbaceous vegetation and having a dry climate.

Most of the forest zone is coniferous and is sometimes called, especially with reference to Siberia, the taiga. But in European Russia a wedge of mixed forest, coniferous and deciduous, stretches south of the coniferous belt from the western frontier and tapers off near Kazan on the Volga. Though smaller in area, the mixed forest is important as the cradle of the modern state, where Russia, centred on Moscow, made a second beginning after the decline of the old Russian state based on Kiev. Besides Moscow itself the area of mixed forest includes such other historic cities as Novgorod, Nizhny Novgorod (now Gorky), Yaroslavl, Vladimir, Smolensk and St Petersburg (now Leningrad).

To travel southwards is not to be struck by any abrupt change from forest to steppe. First comes a transitional area, part woods and part steppe, sometimes termed the wooded steppe or meadow-grass steppe – as found, for example in Oryol Province, scene of Turgenev's *Sportsman's Sketches*. South of that is the steppe proper, also called feather-grass steppe, which in turn blends into arid (also called saline or wormwood) steppe, merging further to the south-east with the sand or stone deserts of Central Asia.

Thinly populated and unfit for cultivation, the arid steppe was the preserve of pastoral nomads. But the steppe proper and the wooded steppe are fertile crop-raising country, coinciding partly with the black earth (*chernozem*) belt which stretches from the western frontier to the Altay foothills and reaches its greatest breadth of just under two hundred miles in European Russia. This became famous as one of the world's granaries and was supporting about a hundred people to the square mile in the early twentieth century. For many centuries, however, the cultivation of these lands had been delayed by the incursions of raiding horsemen, and insufficient rainfall made the raising of crops somewhat hazardous even on black earth.

CLIMATE   Poor agricultural conditions, the attacks of outside enemies, unsettled internal conditions and the exactions of central authority – all tended to make mere survival an achievement. There was also the Russian climate, which, as Yepikhodov says in Chekhov's *Cherry Orchard* (1903–4), 'isn't exactly co-operative'.

Russia has an arctic climate in the extreme north, a subtropical climate in parts of the Black Sea coast, of Transcaucasia and of Central Asia, and a monsoon-type climate on the Pacific coast of the Far East. Such are the fringes. The rest of the country, by far the greatest part of Russian territory, has a continental climate with long, cold winters and short, fairly hot summers. As one travels from west to east the range of temperature, between the cold of winter and the heat of summer, becomes ever wider until the coastal zone is reached. Eastern Siberia has an extreme continental climate. It can have heat waves in summer, with attendant mosquitoes, but its winters are phenomenally severe, and it contains a small town, Verkhoyansk, often claimed as the cold pole of the northern hemisphere, with its mean temperature of −58°F. in January and a lowest recorded temperature of −83·6°F. In most of European Russia too winter is the longest and perhaps the most typically Russian season. The average number of days on which the thermometer falls below freezing point has been put at a hundred and forty and a hundred and fifty in Moscow and St Petersburg respectively, with a hundred and eighty in the middle Urals and a hundred and ninety in Archangel in the far north. Even in the southern port of Odessa the figure is as high as ninety (Schlesinger, p. 238).

SEASONS The Russian winter is monotonous, but awesome and picturesque. It is rendered more tolerable by a tendency for the coldest days to be windless, at least in the north and centre. In the south blizzards are more prevalent, and southern winters too can be severe. For Moscow and St Petersburg society, however, winter was a cheerful season with visits to the theatre and balls, and with sleighs whirring through the streets almost silent on the snow except for the tinkling of their bells. On fine days the low sun glittered blindingly on snow and ice. In winter merchants could transport heavy loads more easily than over the atrocious ruts and mire of the roads in spring and autumn. For the peasants field work came to an end in winter, but many obtained seasonal employment in the towns. Others busied themselves at home, the organisation of cottage industries being widely developed.

The onset of winter, with the arrival of the 'new road' – for sledges instead of carts – was a glad occasion, bringing the end of autumn slush. Yet more exhilarating was the advent of spring, when winter's bleak, silent monochrome rapidly yielded to colours, scents and birdsong, while the breaking ice on the rivers thundered like an artillery barrage. For the farmer the summer was all too short, the sowing and reaping of his crop often being crowded into a mere hundred days. Spurts of intense effort were therefore necessary at sowing, haymaking and harvest time, by contrast to the long periods of winter inactivity.

4 Communications

WATERWAYS   The rivers of European Russia were linked by canals constructed in the eighteenth and nineteenth centuries, especially in the 1810s, and there was thus communication by water between the Black, Caspian, Baltic and White Seas. A cargo ship could make its way from Astrakhan to St Petersburg with a load of seven hundred tons, covering some two thousand five hundred miles of water in forty days. But grain shipments from the south, being compelled to set off in autumn, might be overtaken by winter and reach distant destinations only in the next year. A convoy of seven or eight barges might take four thousand tons of wheat up to the Volga from Samara (now Kuybyshev) to Rybinsk, where it would be stored until spring and then shipped on to St Petersburg (Westwood, p. 18).

Steamships first appeared on the Neva as early as 1815 and were plying on the Volga and Dnieper by the 1820s, but it was not until the end of the century that they were widely used. Before that, traction on the rivers was supplied by men and horses, horses being the more expensive. Teams of 'Volga boatmen' hauled barges upstream by rope, or a tug attached to a train of barges would be warped up-river to an anchor taken ahead by rowing boat, the anchor rope being attached to a capstan turned by horses or teams of men.

Waterways remained the most important channel for transporting freight in bulk over a large part of the country, and were in increasing use throughout the century, despite the development of railways and some improvement in roads. By the early twentieth century Russia had over a hundred thousand miles of navigable inland waterways, carrying over thirty million tons of freight a year, as opposed to six million in 1861. Timber and firewood made up more than half the freight, and grain about an eighth.

Rivers also carried human freight. Part of the journey to prison and penal settlement in Siberia was handled by contractors who conveyed convicts by barge from Tyumen to Tomsk, taking them down the Irtysh and up the Ob (Kennan, p. 83). These vessels were often overloaded, and their tightly packed cargo proved perishable. But for travellers less pressed river transport was the most soothing form of journey with the occasional drama of running aground to relieve the gentle monotony.

According to one nineteenth-century observer, some captains used to carry a few 'stalwart Cossacks' free, so that they could jump overboard when the boat became stranded and pull it off 'with a stout hawser' (Mackenzie Wallace, i, p. 10). The same observer also complains of bugs on the Don steamers, of rats on the Sea of Azov and of an atmosphere of general squalor. The traveller by road was no less exposed to dirt and vermin, however, and river travel was usually considered preferable.

ROADS Road haulage was mainly by horse-power, despite the immemorial camels of the east and the electric trams which were running in St Petersburg from 1880. Conditions were notoriously bad, a typical road being immensely broad, surfaced by nature only, and more a collection of ruts than a highway. Since carriages and carts – even those used by passengers – commonly lacked springs, travellers would take a load of pillows, or hay might be packed in to lessen jolting. Hard-surface high-roads, called *chaussées*, were few indeed. Halfway through the nineteenth century Russia had only three thousand miles of them, and during the Crimean War the Russian army in the south was more effectively cut off from its home bases than were the British and French. Even by the end of the century the Empire had only ten thousand miles of metalled highway.

Two Russian roads were famous. The spectacular Georgian Military Road was travelled by Pushkin in 1829, as is described in his *Journey to Erzerum*. It runs for a hundred and twenty miles through the Daryal Pass in the high Caucasus from Vladikavkaz (now Ordzhonikidze) in the north to Tiflis in the south. The other was remarkable for its length of some four thousand miles and for the misfortunes of the many exiles and convicts who trod or rode it. It led from St Petersburg through Novgorod, Moscow, Nizhny Novgorod and Kazan to Perm. Entering Siberia, it became the Siberian Highway and proceeded as far as Irkutsk. Chekhov, who travelled along it through Tyumen and Tomsk in 1890, called it the longest and ugliest road in the world.

In *Eugene Onegin* Pushkin describes a road journey made by the Larin family in central European Russia, from a country estate to Moscow, and lists some of the disadvantages. Perhaps, he says, Russia may have a network of *chaussées*, iron bridges and underwater tunnels in five hundred years' time. But 'now our roads are bad. Neglected bridges rot. At post-stations you can't get a minute's sleep for bugs and fleas. There are no inns – just a pretentious, but meagre menu hanging in a cold hut for appearance's sake and mocking your futile appetite.' However, he goes on to point out that, 'travelling in the cold season of winter is pleasant and easy' (Pushkin, *Eugene Onegin* vii, verses 33–5).

Winter travel indeed was a comparatively salubrious experience. With a carpet of snow and ice covering the greater part of the Empire, one could sleigh from the northern port of Archangel on the White Sea to the Caspian port of Astrakhan at the mouth of the Volga, even if many of the 'roads' consisted only of a row of posts to show the way. But winter travel too had its disadvantages. Passengers could experience nausea from swooping up and down undulations in the snow. Open sledges were used, an ordeal in Siberian conditions, especially with a head wind – even if some found it pleasurably exciting to be tumbled out when, as often happened, the sledge overturned into soft snow.

Many travellers have commented on the unsavoury post-stations, where one was lucky to find room on a bench or on the floor to rest for an hour or two while other journeyers chatted, laughed, smoked, drank, swore and scratched themselves. Post-stations were set up at intervals of ten to twenty miles along the main roads and made it possible, though not always easy, to resume one's journey on producing the *podorozhnaya*; this was a large warrant stamped with the imperial eagle and entitling the traveller to the horses, carriage and driver which would convey him to the next post-station against a fixed tariff. In practice, as Russian literature testifies, travellers were often greeted at the door by the postmaster with a rude bellow: 'No horses!' But tact, bribery, patience or bullying would produce them in the end. There is a picture of these conditions in *The Postmaster*, one of Pushkin's *Tales of Belkin* (1831), beginning: 'Who has not cursed postmasters, who has not quarrelled with them?'

In a country so rich in waterways, bridges formed a notorious hazard to the land traveller. Mackenzie Wallace calls them a barrier, not a connecting link, and says that the cautious driver would prefer to take to the water if it could be forded. He has a vivid description of a Russian coachman negotiating a bridge.

Making hurriedly the sign of the Cross, he gathers up his reins, waves his little whip in the air, and, shouting lustily, urges on his team. The operation is not wanting in excitement. First there is a short descent; then the horses plunge wildly through a zone of deep mud; next comes a fearful jolt as the vehicle is jerked up on to the first planks; then the transverse planks, which are but loosely held in their places, rattle and rumble ominously, as the experienced, sagacious animals pick their way cautiously and gingerly among the dangerous holes and crevices; lastly you plunge with a horrible jolt into a second mud zone, and finally regain *terra firma*, conscious of that pleasant sensation which a young officer may be supposed to feel after his first cavalry charge in real warfare (Mackenzie Wallace, i, p. 23).

Privileged travellers naturally progressed more rapidly, and we have figures on the time taken by various Tsars to cover the four hundred and eighty-six miles from St Petersburg to Moscow in winter conditions. For many years Peter the Great's record stood at forty-eight hours, but was lowered to forty-two by Alexander I in 1810. In December 1833, according to a note in Pushkin's journal, Nicholas I beat all records by covering the distance in thirty-eight hours (Pushkin, *Eugene Onegin*, ed. Nabokov, iii, p. 112).

How difficult a feat journeys could be for less august wayfarers is illustrated by many masterpieces of Russian travel literature in addition to some already mentioned. They include Chekhov's journey across Siberia to Sakhalin, described in his letters and the articles *From Siberia* (1890) written *en route*. A trans-Siberian haul in the opposite direction at the time of the Crimean War, from Ayan on the Sea of Okhotsk to Yakutsk, is described in the closing chapters of Goncharov's *Frigate Pallas*. To them may be added two classics of English and American nineteenth-century travel: *Ride to Khiva* by Captain Fred Burnaby of the Royal Horse Guards (1876) and George Kennan's *Siberia and the Exile System* (1891). Among numerous evocations of the Russian road in fiction are the two journeys, one fatal, the other uproarious, in Tolstoy's *Master and Man* (1895) and Gogol's *Dead Souls* respectively.

RAILWAYS   The first public railway in Russia, between St Petersburg and nearby Tsarskoye Selo (now Pushkin), the Tsar's residence, was opened in 1837. The Warsaw–Vienna line, the second
to receive Nicholas I's approval, ran outside the boundaries of
Russia proper, but was opened opportunely in 1848 in time to carry
the Russian troops used in the following year to suppress the Hungarian uprising. The first major Russian railway was the St Petersburg–Moscow line, opened in 1851. This runs in an almost straight
line between the two cities, but the story that Nicholas I settled a
dispute about its course by ruler and pen, even including four small
kinks where his fingers stuck out over the edge of the ruler, is
probably untrue (Westwood, p. 30).

At the time of the Crimean War Russia had only seven hundred
and fifty miles of railway. The first Russian railway boom took place
in the 1860s and early 1870s, leaving the Empire with over 14,000
miles of track in 1881. This was mainly the work of private firms
operating under government guarantee. A further boom, including the construction of the Trans-Siberian Railway, took place
between 1891 and 1905, adding nearly 20,000 miles of new line.
The second Russian railway boom was more of a state enterprise,
and the treasury had also begun to buy up privately owned railway
companies.

Russian trains were large, being built to a wider gauge than those
of western Europe. Foreigners found them comfortable, but slow
and unpunctual. As protection against the intense cold they had
double windows and doors, and they were heated by iron stoves.
All carriages could be used as sleepers and there were three classes,
the third having wooden benches. Stations were often placed in-
conveniently far from the towns which they were designed to serve,
as is often noted in Chekhov's stories and plays. As he explains,
town councils could not always raise the large bribes which
engineers and constructors required before they would agree to
locate the stations more conveniently – and in any case land was
cheaper outside the towns.

One practice often mentioned in literature has outlived imperial
Russia – that of ringing the station bell three times before a train
left. The first (single) ring took place a quarter of an hour before
departure, the second (double) ring gave five minutes' warning, and
on the third (triple) peal the train pulled out.

Tolstoy's Anna Karenin committed suicide by throwing herself

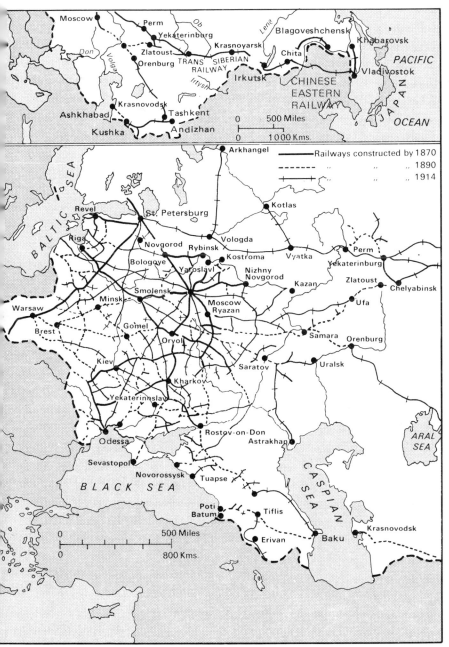

3 *The Imperial Russian Railway System*, showing the extent of the permanent way in 1870, 1890 and 1914. The first major Russian railway was the St Petersburg–Moscow line, opened in 1851. Booms in railway building took place in the 1860s and early 1870s; and also between 1891 and 1905, during which time a large part of the Trans-Siberian Railway was built.

under a train, thereby disrupting the casual and companionable conventions of the Russian railway ethos. On more normal occasions the conductor's samovar would be steaming away to provide unlimited tea. Or passengers would make their own, queuing up during halts at stations to take boiling water available in large cauldrons.

Russian industrialisation of the late nineteenth century owed much to the railways, but they never caught the popular imagination as in North America. Russian railway building has been called a 'forced growth sponsored by the Tsar and built by foreigners' (Westwood, p. 7). This is perhaps to exaggerate, but it is true that the state provided much of the initiative and finance, including the proceeds of selling Alaska to the United States in 1867.

5 Peoples

A MULTINATIONAL STATE   Western Europeans of the nineteenth century often maintained that there were too many Russians in the world. Writing in the 1880s, when the population stood at about 115 million, Leroy-Beaulieu pointed out that Russia had twice as many citizens as the most populous among the other Christian countries (Leroy-Beaulieu, i, p. 5). In 1900 a Russian authority on military affairs called the Empire's reserves of manpower 'downright inexhaustible', and warned that it could easily maintain a standing army of two and a half million should it wish to make 'as great an effort as certain western European states' (Kovalevsky, p. 953). Population, by territorial expansion and natural increase, was growing fast from about thirty-six million in 1796 to the nearly one hundred and twenty-six million, excluding Finland with over two and a half million, recorded in the census of 1897 – an increase of three and a half times in a century. Leroy-Beaulieu had earlier calculated that the population would reach one hundred and eighty million by about 1950, but underestimated (Leroy-Beaulieu, i, p. 41).

By no means were all the Empire's citizens Russians, though foreigners often assumed that they were, just as the same natural mistake is still made about citizens of the Soviet Union, and just as the uninitiated insist on regarding Scotsmen, Welshmen and Irishmen as English. The person whom the untutored foreigner called a Russian might in fact be a Lithuanian peasant, a Georgian prince, a nomad Kalmuck, a Tungus from eastern Siberia or a Polish count. Some of these, not least the Polish count, would be quick to correct the error. Others might not bother, while some from the remotest parts might rarely have set eyes on Russians and know them only by repute.

The Empire contained a mixture of races professing many

religions and speaking a profusion of tongues, but our brief survey of these complexities must be russocentric, and no attempt will be made even to list all the numerous peoples and their languages. The Slavs, who formed the core of the population, will be considered first, and after them the non-Slav peoples.

THE EAST SLAVS   Apart from the Poles (considered below, p. 51), the Slavs of the Empire belonged to the East Slav branch. They are now three distinct peoples: Russians, Ukrainians and Belorussians. In the nineteenth century this distinction was less clear, however, and many of those who would now be called Ukrainians and Belorussians were simply regarded as Russians, being so designated by imperial officials, foreign historians and guide-books such as Baedeker's.

Under the Tsars the Ukrainians were officially known as Little Russians and the Ukraine was called Little Russia. The term Ukraine goes back at least to the seventeenth century, but it was not until the nineteenth century, and under the influence of an active national movement, that Ukrainians began to call themselves such. Besides those who simply thought of themselves as Russian, many also considered themselves Cossacks, and they used the term Muscovites (*moskali*) to describe Russians in the more restricted sense, otherwise known as Great Russians. In return Muscovites called them 'top-knots' (*khokhly*).

The term Great Russian is literary, not colloquial, and was used in the nineteenth century to describe those who are now simply called Russians, when it was necessary to differentiate them from Ukrainians and Belorussians. It is still sometimes convenient to use the term Great Russian to avoid confusion, and it is literature written in the Great Russian language – not the literature of the Ukraine or Belorussia – to which the present study presents a background. The Belorussians are, incidentally, sometimes referred to as White Russians, which is natural since Russian *bely* means 'white', but can lead to confusion owing to the use of the same term to describe the opponents of the Reds in the Russian Civil War of 1917–22, and also decreasingly to describe emigrants from the USSR in general.

One further point must be stressed. Nationality was more closely associated with religion in the nineteenth century than it is in the officially anti-religious Soviet Union. Any subject of the Tsar, professing the Orthodox faith, tended to be considered a Russian, whatever his racial origin, if he spoke Russian as his first language. Religion, language, domicile and citizenship made a Russian. Racial origin, the shape of eyes, nose and cheekbones, even skin pigmentation – these were unimportant.

In the old Russian state based on Kiev between the ninth and thirteenth centuries, there had been tribal distinctions, but none significantly corresponding to the present distinctions between Great Russian, Ukrainian and Belorussian. These are the result of separate historical evolution since Kievan times and owe much to the fact that the ancestors of the Ukrainians and Belorussians came under the Tatars briefly or not at all, but were under Lithuanian and Polish rule for several centuries.

The relative numbers of the three peoples are shown by the census of 1897, at which time the total population of the Empire stood at about 128 million:

	Nineteenth-century name	Population	Modern name
	Great Russian	c. 55·7 million	Russian
	Little Russian	c. 22·4 million	Ukrainian
	Belorussian	c. 5·9 million	Belorussian
TOTAL:	Russians (as qualified above)	c. 84·0 million	

Great Russians, Ukrainians and Belorussians together formed about two-thirds of the population at the end of the nineteenth century. Great Russians on their own came to about 45 per cent of the total – and were themselves, accordingly, a minority people.

MUSCOVY AND IMPERIAL RUSSIA   Moscow began its career as an 'appanage' princedom dependent on the nearby great princedom of Vladimir. But the princes of Moscow gradually absorbed neighbouring territory, aided by their central geographical position and convenient access to the main river routes. This process was well advanced by 1480, the year in which Moscow is regarded as having ceased to pay tribute to the Tatars, thus formally becoming the centre of an independent state. Muscovy continued to expand. Before the accession of Ivan the Terrible in 1533 it had taken over all other previously autonomous Russian territories except those ruled by Lithuania and Poland. Ivan assumed the title Tsar of All Russia in 1547 and greatly extended Muscovite control by conquering

Tatar lands in Kazan, Astrakhan and Siberia. Further expansion
into Siberia and the incorporation of part of the Ukraine followed
in the seventeenth century.

Proclaimed the first Russian Emperor in 1721, Peter the Great
launched the imperial period of Russian history. He transformed
and modernised the country, replacing Moscow as capital with the
newly founded St Petersburg in 1712. Renamed Petrograd in 1914,
this remained the capital until 1918, when Moscow resumed its old
status. But Moscow had never entirely lost its special position, as
was symbolised by the practice of referring to 'the two capitals'.

UKRAINIANS Ukrainians had an especially turbulent history,
being ruled by, quarrelled over and partitioned among Turks, Poles,
Austrians and Great Russians, rebelling and intriguing against all,
and falling gradually within the expanding Russian state. If
Ukrainians must be ruled by others, it was the Great Russians, also
members of the Orthodox Church, whom they preferred. In 1654
the Ukrainian Cossack Bogdan Khmelnitsky, leader of a successful
revolt against Poland, brought large parts of the Ukraine into union
with Muscovy. There was argument later about the degree of
autonomy accorded to Ukrainians under this arrangement. In any
case they were incorporated in the imperial state in the reign of
Catherine the Great, when the three partitions of Poland brought
Belorussia and the remaining Polish-ruled parts of the Ukraine
within the Russian Empire, except Galicia, which went to Austria.

Catherine's reign also saw Russian rule established over large territories on the Black Sea coast, including the Crimea, which had
been under Turkish control. Called New Russia, a name now obso-
lete, these provinces were colonised by Ukrainians, Russians and
others including Greeks, Bulgarians and Germans. The Ukrainians,
who suffered from overpopulation, helped to colonise the Ukraine,
and Ukrainian officers became serf-owning aristocrats admitted to
the status of gentry in Russian law.

Ukrainian nationalism, aspiring to autonomy within the Empire
or to full independence, arose in the 1840s under the influence of
the Ukrainian poet Taras Shevchenko. The Polish revolt of 1863
led the Russian government to restrict local cultures, and from 1876
to 1905 it was illegal to publish anything in Ukrainian except folk-
lore material. Is Ukrainian an independent language or a mere dialect of Russian? The former, surely, but the question has exercised

both Ukrainians and Russians, often being judged more by political than linguistic criteria. Among the great Russian writers Gogol was of Ukrainian origin, and his two early collections of stories, *Evenings on a Farm near Dikanka* (1831–2) and *Mirgorod* (1835), are set in the Ukraine and draw on Ukrainian folk-lore and history, but are written in Russian.

COSSACKS As reference to Gogol reminds us, Cossacks often figure in Russian literature. They were not a separate people, but Russians or Ukrainians who absorbed other ethnic elements as well, being mainly descendants of peasants of Orthodox faith, who had fled to the frontiers to escape serfdom, taxes and (in the case of those evading Polish rule) religious and national persecution.

Cossack (*kazak*) comes from a Turkic word meaning 'free man, warrior', and their original communities had arisen by the sixteenth century on the Rivers Dnieper, Don and Ural (then called Yaik) as self-governing bodies engaged in hunting, fishing, pillaging and conducting guerrilla warfare against Turk and Tatar. In the seventeenth century they turned to agriculture. The same century also saw the revolt of Stenka Razin (1670), followed just over a hundred years later by that of Pugachov (1773), the participants in both uprisings being largely Cossacks. Pushkin wrote a *History of the Pugachov Rebellion* (1834) and brought Pugachov and his revolt into the novel *The Captain's Daughter* (1836). The most famous Cossack community was the 'Sech' of the Zaporozhian Cossacks on the lower Dnieper, which is described by Gogol in *Taras Bulba* (1835), set in the seventeenth century. The Sech was abolished by Catherine the Great in 1775, and its chief *ataman* (leader) Kalnishevsky was immured in the Solovetsky Monastery.

As this indicates, the state severely regimented the once free Cossacks in the eighteenth century, when they also began to be used as more regular frontier forces. Cossack communities were founded by the central government in the north Caucasus, in the areas of Astrakhan and Orenburg, and in parts of Siberia. Cossack leaders, once elected in popular assembly, and senior officers, came to be appointed by the Tsar or war ministry and the Cossacks acquired their own landowning aristocracy. The Don Cossacks were their chief community, supplying in the early twentieth century seventeen of the thirty-five Cossack regiments in the peacetime Russian army. The Cossacks became pillars of the state, regarded as the

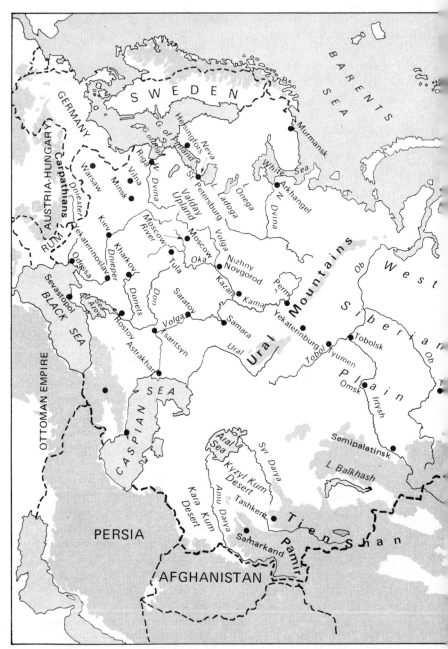

4 *Russia in Asia:* administrative boundaries (late nineteenth century). Since
population density was so much less than in European Russia, the administrative
areas are correspondingly larger; the Yakutsk Region was the biggest of all and
larger than many European states.

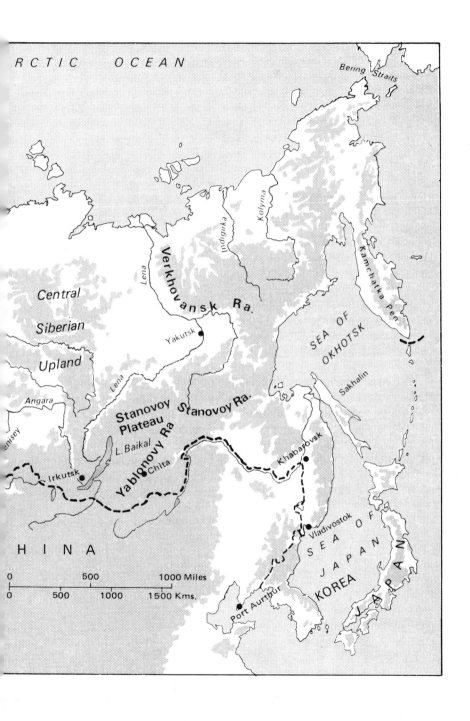

Tsar's most loyal soldiers and used as riot police to suppress political and labour disorders. They performed compulsory military service, each providing his own horse and equipment in return for privileges which included tax exemption.

Their romantic past as turbulent pioneers of a Russian 'wild east' made the Cossacks picturesque figures to compatriots in the hinterland, who could read a vivid contemporary account of them in Tolstoy's *Cossacks* in addition to the historical fiction and other works of Pushkin and Gogol mentioned above.

SIBERIA   Siberia usually denoted the Russian Empire east of the Urals, excluding Central Asia. Though containing many indigenous peoples, it became predominantly Slav after colonisation had begun in the sixteenth century, when Russians probed these vast territories in search of salt, fish and furs. In 1581 the mercantile family of the Stroganovs mounted an expedition led by the Cossack Yermak, who achieved the conquest of Siberia by defeating a local ruler, the Siberian Khan Kuchum. In 1639 another Cossack, Ivan Moskvityanin, reached the Pacific Ocean.

The Siberian tribes were defenceless against Russian expansion, but many still survived, including the Buryats (Buddhists or Christians who speak a language akin to Mongol); the Yakuts (who speak a Turkic language); and the partly nomad, hunting, fishing, reindeer-hunting Tunguses and Chuckchis.

Since the eighteenth century Siberia has been a place of exile and imprisonment for criminal and political offenders, including a number of writers. Siberians enjoyed more freedom than European Russians – partly because none of them could be 'sent to Siberia' (since they were already there), and partly because the institution of serfdom did not operate there.

Siberia had a population much smaller than that of European Russia, but it was growing faster, from just over a million in 1800 to the five and three quarter million recorded in the 1897 census. Towards the end of the century these vast territories were increasingly colonised, especially in the west, by settlers from overpopulated parts of southern Great Russia and the Ukraine. The movement enjoyed a varying degree of official support, and after the famine of 1891 and the building of the Trans-Siberian Railway, mainly in 1891–9, the number of immigrants swelled to over a hundred thousand a year. In parts of Siberia peasants could find steppe, including black earth, in conditions resembling those of their old homes. Would-be immigrants were at one time obliged to send scouts ahead to pick land which could be reserved until the main body arrived.

Dostoyevsky's *Memoirs from the House of the Dead* contains a celebrated account of Siberia, and portrays his own experiences, thinly disguised as fiction, as a convict serving a four-year sentence in the prison at Omsk. Vladimir Korolenko also drew on Siberian experiences, as an exile to the remote Yakutsk Region, in his story *Makar's Dream* (1885). Missionary activity in eastern Siberia forms the theme of Leskov's story *On the Edge of the World* (1889), based on the real-life experiences of Nil, Archbishop of Irkutsk; and the hero of Tolstoy's *Resurrection* follows the heroine to Siberia. To the nineteenth-century literature of Siberia must be added Chekhov's sociological study *Sakhalin Island* (1893) and other writings referred to above (p. 39).

POLES   Areas which, according to one's point of view, were Russian, Polish, Belorussian, Jewish or Ukrainian were brought into the Russian Empire by the partitions of Poland at the end of the eighteenth century, and the greater part of the Duchy of Warsaw, including Warsaw itself, followed after the Congress of Vienna (1814–15). Known in Russian as the Polish Tsardom, this came under harsher Russian control after the Polish insurrections which broke out in 1830 and 1863, and could only be quelled by major military campaigns resulting in the exile of many Poles to Siberia. The Poles were proud of their national culture and Catholic religion, and felt that Poland was entitled to large tracts of territory which Russians looked on as theirs. The two comic Poles in Dostoyevsky's *Brothers Karamazov* accordingly refuse to drink a toast to Russia without the reservation 'in its boundaries before 1772'. As an extreme Russian nationalist, Dostoyevsky often brought in such 'absurd little Poles' as minor characters. In a more truculent spirit, Pushkin had taken the opportunity of the Polish revolt of 1830 to warn western Europeans not to meddle in inter-Slav quarrels in his great denunciatory lyric *To Russia's Calumniators* (1831). Poland brought out the chauvinist in many Russians, but the Poles found some support among liberal-minded Russians, of whom Herzen was one. A late story by Tolstoy, *What for?* (1906), gives a sympathetic presentation of the Poles involved in the insurrection of 1830–1,

providing a pleasant contrast with Pushkin's harshness. At the end
of the century the number of Poles in the Empire was about nine
million.

NON-SLAVS (GENERAL)   About a third of the Empire's population
consisted of non-Slavs, among whom Turkic peoples, recorded as
over fourteen million in the 1897 census, were most numerous –
about eleven per cent of the total. Finnic peoples amounted to some
five and a half million, almost equalled by the Jews. Other non-
Slav peoples, numbering over a million at the end of the century,
were Germans, Armenians, Georgians, Latvians, Lithuanians and
Rumanians.

TURKIC-SPEAKING AND MUSLIM PEOPLES   Turkey itself was an
independent state often in conflict with Russia, but the Russian
Empire contained large groups speaking Turkic languages. Among
these were the Tatars, closely linked with the Russians from early
times. Some English proverbs impute ferocity to the Tatar, but
those of nineteenth-century Russia were known for their sobriety and
domestic virtues, being more commonly engaged in peaceful agriculture than in slitting throats. They were used in positions of trust,
as watchmen, caretakers and domestic servants, and fashionable St
Petersburg restaurants used to recruit waiters from the Tatars of
Ryazan Province.

   Earlier Tatars had been more adept with bow and arrow than
with napkin and corkscrew, being indeed of wilder origin than their
sober nineteenth-century occupations suggest. They were descendants of the raiding horsemen who formed the invading armies of
the Golden Horde, the Mongol-Tatar state set up in the thirteenth
century by Batu Khan, a grandson of Genghis Khan. Reaching the
Volga in 1236 after huge conquests to east and south, they overran
most of old Russia during the next four years and kept it under tribute, but not occupation, for nearly two and a half centuries. To
this period the terms Mongol invasion and Tatar yoke are both
applied, indicating that two distinct peoples were involved. In fact
the Mongols were a small ruling class, and it was Turkic-speaking
peoples, later called Tatars, who supplied the bulk of the armies
and assimilated the ruling Mongol minority.

   The Tatars were converted to Islam and formed separate states
(Khanates) of which the two most important were those of the Cri-

mea and Kazan – the latter conquered by Russia in the sixteenth century, as were also the Tatar Khanates of Astrakhan and Siberia.

Tatars and Russians lived side by side on the Volga and elsewhere, some assimilation taking place, and though difference of religion hindered the process, certain ruling Tatar families founded aristocratic lines as Russian princes. The Crimean Khanate, at first independent, became part of the Ottoman Empire in the fifteenth century, and it was not until 1783 that Russia annexed the Crimea. One popular Russian work set in Tatar Crimea was Pushkin's poem, *The Fountain of Bakhchisaray* (1824).

In the nineteenth century the term Tatar was applied to the Kazan (or Volga) Tatars, numbering 1·7 million in the 1897 census, who may be considered the descendants of Batu's Golden Horde. It was also given to the Transcaucasian Tatars (as they were then called), numbering some two million – the ancestors of the modern Azerbaydzhanis; and also to the Crimean Tatars, numbering about two hundred thousand, and to the small group of Siberian Tatars living in western Siberia.

Confusion can be created when the word Tatar is loosely applied to all Muslim inhabitants of the Russian Empire, most of whom were also Turkic-speaking. There were some twelve million Muslims in all at the beginning of the twentieth century. Many had been brought in recently through Russian conquests in Central Asia during the second half of the nineteenth century – Turkmens, Uzbeks, Kara-Kalpaks and many others.

It is impossible to trace all these peoples in a brief study, especially as comment is bedevilled by more recent developments and by complex changes of name and frontier. As an indication of these intricacies we may take one of the most numerous Muslim, Turkic-speaking (but not Tatar) peoples of the nineteenth century – the Kirgiz-Kaysaks, who correspond to the modern Kazakhs but not, as might be thought, to the modern Kirgiz, the main inhabitants of the present-day Union Republic of Kirgizia (known in the nineteenth century as the Kara-Kirgiz). The Kara-Kirgiz too were Muslim and Turkic-speaking, but less numerous – probably less than two hundred thousand to some four million of the Kirgiz-Kaysaks, who wandered the steppes of east European and Central Asiatic Russia. A period as a prisoner of the nomad Kirgiz forms one of the hero's adventures in Leskov's *Enchanted Wanderer* (1873).

The Bashkirs, another Turkic-speaking and Muslim people, were of mixed Finno-Ugrian and Turkic origin, with a Mongolian admixture too. They numbered over half a million in the early twentieth century – agriculturalists and nomads who lived in the south Urals in the area of the present Autonomous Republic of Bashkiria. The Bashkir steppe and Ufa, the main town, are the scene of S.T. Aksakov's family reminiscences disguised as fiction, *Family Chronicle* and *The Childhood of Bagrov the Grandson*. The Chuvash of the middle Volga, the area which is now the Chuvash Autonomous Republic, were another Turkic-speaking people, but were unusual in practising Orthodox Christianity by contrast with the Muslim affiliations of most Turkic-speakers.

MONGOLIAN PEOPLES Russia had two Mongolian-speaking peoples of Buddhist religion, one in Europe and one in Asia. Of these the Buryats of south-eastern Siberia have been mentioned above. The others were the Kalmucks, nomads of the lower Volga, who numbered about one hundred and thirty thousand in the early twentieth century, when they roamed the arid steppes with their tents, camels and flocks. They somewhat resembled the Chinese in appearance and were easily distinguished from Tatars. Their religious leader was a Grand Lama, who came to be appointed by the Russian Tsar from the beginning of the twentieth century. They enjoyed local autonomy under the governor of Astrakhan.

FINNIC PEOPLES Finland was part of the Russian Empire between 1808–9, when it was annexed from Sweden, and 1917, when it obtained independence. Between these dates it enjoyed internal autonomy with its own laws and a sense of national identity, being ruled as a Grand Duchy, separate from the Empire as a whole and under a governor-general appointed by the Tsar. The impact of the small Russian population, only about six thousand at the beginning of the twentieth century, was slight. The Finns of Finland numbered over two and a half million at the end of the nineteenth century. Finnish scenery, and the misfortunes of a Finnish girl seduced by a Russian officer, form themes in the poem *Eda* (1824–5) by Ye. A. Baratynsky. But Finland, though under Russian control, was regarded as a foreign country, and it does not figure prominently in the main works of Russian nineteenth-century literature, which tended to be russocentric.

Apart from the Finns of Finland, whose frontier reached to St

Petersburg, there were many Finnish villages on Russian soil in the region of the capital. This was sometimes spoken of as a Russian island in a Finnish sea, though the Russians of St Petersburg greatly outnumbered the Finns around them. Not far away to the west the Estonians, totalling nearly a million in the late nineteenth century, represented another branch of the Baltic Finns.

It was not the Baltic Finns who most affected Russian evolution, but their kinsmen resident on Russian territory and belonging to the wider grouping termed Finnic. The Baltic Finns form only one subdivision of these, admittedly the most advanced and nationally self-conscious. To the Finnic groups also belonged many pockets of peoples on different cultural levels, scattered about the country. They showed varying degrees of assimilation with the dominant Slavs, with each other, and with Turkic and other peoples.

Finnic tribes were the earlier occupants of the forests centred on Moscow which became the cradle of the Great Russian state. To what extent was this sparse population annihilated, driven out or absorbed by the advancing Slav? This remains problematic, but the general agreement is that it was to a great extent absorbed. It has been asserted that the Great Russians, as opposed to the Ukrainians and Belorussians, tend to have Finnic physical features, in particular flat faces with high cheekbones. The Finnic tribes, too, left behind many place names in areas which seemed to be purely Great Russian. The very name Moscow (*Moskva*), though of disputed etymology, has been considered Finnic. Moreover, as several nineteenth-century observers have illustrated, it was possible to find Finnic villages in every stage of linguistic and cultural assimilation. Yet there are surprisingly few Finnic loan-words in Russian. So far as cultural influence is concerned, the Finns found it more blessed to receive than to give.

There were Finnic settlements along the Volga from Nizhny Novgorod to Samara – those of the Mordva, scattered over a larger area than that of the present-day Mordva Autonomous Republic, and of the Cheremis, now called Mari, situated in the area of the present-day Mari Autonomous Republic. Further east, near Perm, were the Finnic Votyaks (now called Udmurts) and the Zyryans and Permyaks (now called Komi and Komi-Permyaks respectively). Two small peoples, the Ostyaks (now called Khanty) and Voguls (now called Mansi) further complicate the picture by being of Ugrian origin, that is, belonging to the larger and more nebulous category of Finno–Ugrians, to which the Magyars of Hungary belong. Most of these peoples had been converted to the Orthodox faith, which assisted their assimilation by the Russians. The Finnic peoples abandoned their original primitive religion for Orthodox Christianity and were thus more easily absorbed by Russians than the Turkic peoples, who tended to retain their Muslim faith.

The conversion of Finnic peoples to Orthodoxy was not always as smooth as Russians liked to picture it. Herzen describes how the Russian police and clergy combined to blackmail the Votyaks in the area of Perm. Every few years a police officer and a priest would tour the villages to check how many Votyaks had been going to church, for they still hankered after their old, pagan religion, though supposedly converted to Orthodoxy. Herzen says that they were flogged, fined and put in prison, while the 'spiritual detective and earthly missionary . . . raise a huge ransom . . . then go away, leaving everything as it was, so as to have a chance to come back again a year or two later, with their birch and cross' (*My Past and Thoughts*, ch. xv).

JEWS   As mentioned above, the partitions of Poland at the end of the eighteenth century brought Russia large new territories in the west. With them came a Jewish population estimated at about a million. So far there had been few Jews in Russia, where permanent residence had been denied to them by law, including an edict of 1762.

The Jewish population increased faster than that of the Empire as a whole, and it has been claimed that a half of the total number of Jews in the late nineteenth century were subjects of the Tsar. The Russian government did not find a satisfactory policy for dealing with them, and they became a major social problem, or were made into one by the authorities. Jewish religion, dress, culture, education and language (a dialect of German, the forerunner of modern Yiddish) all seemed to set them apart. They usually had recognisably Jewish names too – yet another factor tending to distinguish the Jews as a separate people. Any tendency towards assimilation was checked by the increasingly severe disabilities imposed on them by the government.

The chief restriction was confinement to a ghetto territory, the so-called pale of settlement, consisting of certain provinces of the western and southern Empire in addition to the Jews' old homes in Poland. Even inside the pale, Jews were required to reside in towns or urban settlements, and not in villages, while in the towns they might be limited to specific quarters, as was the case in Kiev, Sevastopol and Nikolayev. From the resort of Yalta they were entirely banned in the early 1890s. There were exceptions to these residence limitations at certain times, and Jewish communities accordingly grew up in Moscow and St Petersburg. Among those permitted to reside outside the pale were merchants of the First Guild (see p. 121) and their retainers, as well as dispensers, apothecaries and some classes of craftsmen – and also Jews with university degrees. Not that such qualifications were easily achieved, since another disability, imposed in 1887, was a quota for the admission of Jews to institutes of higher learning – ten per cent within the pale, five per cent outside – except that in Moscow and St Petersburg the quota was only three per cent.

Jews were resented for their alien religion and culture, or as commercial rivals, money-lenders, tax-collecting agents, vendors of hard liquor and generally as exploiters. But they were themselves exploited by Russian officials who extorted bribes and treated them as second-class citizens. They were even officially classed, together with certain primitive Asiatic tribes, as aliens (*inorodtsy*; literally 'those of other race'). In addition to their disadvantages in law, many lived in grave poverty in atrocious slums. In the late nineteenth century anti-Jewish riots took place, especially in south and west Russia, including Odessa, and also Kishinyov, where there was a particularly severe pogrom in 1903. These pogroms were directed mainly against property, though fatal casualties were by no means unknown – some fifty persons were killed and several hundred injured in the Kishinyov pogrom. Whether or not the authorities actively encouraged pogroms – and on a local level this clearly did occur – the government could probably have ended them if it had wished.

Jews could escape some of their disabilities by accepting conversion to Orthodox Christianity, which entitled them to 'normal' civil rights – for what that was worth in imperial Russia. But a Jew was always liable to molestation, and a particularly harsh measure was the sudden expulsion from Moscow of about twenty thousand Jews, some two-thirds of the city's Jewish community, in 1891 (Greenberg, ii, p. 44). On a more anecdotal level a British Jew who was also a member of parliament, Sir Samuel Montagu, was once ordered to leave Moscow within twenty-four hours (Clarkson, p. 387), and there was the well-known story of the Jewish girl from the pale who could only pursue her academic studies, which involved residence in St Petersburg, by taking out a 'yellow ticket' – registering herself as a prostitute. It is not surprising that Jews emigrated in large numbers, or that Jewish intellectuals became prominent in the Russian revolutionary movement of the 1890s.

In nineteenth-century Russian literature Jews figure less than their numbers and importance seem to warrant. One reason for this is territorial. Most major literary works are set in Russia outside the pale of settlement and therefore in areas where most Jews could not legally reside. Where Jews do appear, reference to the scene of the action often shows that it is set at some place or time where residence restrictions on Jews did not operate. Thus an early story by Turgenev, *The Jew* (1847), is set in Danzig in 1813 and consists of the war reminiscences of a Russian colonel. Or the scene may be in the Ukraine, as in the seventeenth-century pogrom described with apparent relish by Gogol in *Taras Bulba* – that from which his comic Jewish character Yankel contrives to extricate himself. As this work vividly reminds the reader, the Cossacks were traditionally anti-Semitic.

One leading Russian writer too was strongly anti-Semitic – Dostoyevsky, whose *Diary of a Writer* contains many violent denunciations of the Jews. This attitude is confirmed by his correspondence, but is little reflected in his novels. Jews occasionally figure in Chekhov's stories, for instance the innkeeper Moses in *Steppe* (1888) and a character in *Rothchild's Fiddle* (1894). The plot of his play *Ivanov* (1887–9) hinges on the marriage of a Russian landowner to a Jewish girl, Sarah, who has given up her religion and family and changed her first name to the 'Christian' name Anna.

Besides the Jews of western Russia, imperial expansion also incorporated other much smaller Jewish communities: the Krymchaks of the Crimea, the Georgian Jews, the mountain Jews of the Caucasus and those of Bokhara in Central Asia. These differed from western Jews in speaking the local languages of their areas, and were descended from immigrants of ancient or medieval times.

GERMANS Germans formed an important minority within the Empire, numbering about two million in the early twentieth century, to which must be added some three hundred thousand German or Austrian subjects resident in Russia. Among German subjects of Russia, the Baltic Germans of the provinces of Estland, Livland and Kurland, numbering some three hundred thousand, were an influential group. The majority of the local population consisted of Estonians and Latvians, but Germans were culturally and economically dominant, and included the large landowners. Baltic Germans rose to high rank in the Russian civil service, where they had the reputation of being diehard conservatives and fanatical bureaucrats. This was not always deserved, for not all were Benckendorffs. In any case the anti-German policy adopted by the Russian government in the 1880s caused their influence to decrease. They usually remained Protestant by religion and did not readily assimilate with Russians.

Aloofness was also practised by the German settlers, nearly one million in the early twentieth century, who farmed the lower Volga (the 'Volga Germans'), south European Russia – especially near Odessa – Bessarabia and parts of the Caucasus. Lutheran or Mennonite by religion, these colonists, as they were called, had been officially encouraged to settle in Russia in the late eighteenth and early nineteenth centuries. Their houses, churches and clothes were usually German in style, their settlements and villages had such names as Mannheim and Zürich, and they spoke their native tongue, usually a south German dialect. A typical German farming settlement was a prosperous island within a sea of feckless Slavs, whose agricultural methods and implements were often inferior.

Germans were employed in managerial positions. They were also influential as scholars and scientists working and teaching in Russia, besides which many young Russians, of whom Turgenev was one, studied at German universities. Germans were better known in Russia than any other foreigners, being both admired and resented. Men of action in Russian literature tended to seem implausible unless they were given non-Russian names – preferably German, such as Stolz in Goncharov's *Oblomov*. But Russians also liked to deride the efficient, calculating German, and a classic picture of a comic clash between Teuton and Slav is found in Leskov's story *An Iron Will* (1876) with its memorable picture of a discomfited German, Hugo Karlovich Pektoralis.

Another grotesque story of Slav and Teuton, taken from real life, is told by Herzen about the visit of a certain Count Essen to Vladimir to preside over the induction of conscripts into the army. A peasant elder, desiring some favour, foolishly offered this German general a bribe. But 'unluckily our Count ... was brought up in the school of the Baltic aristocracy, which taught German loyalty to the Russian sovereign'. Count Essen lost his temper, shouted and sent for the gendarmes, and the hapless peasant, who could not conceive of anyone in uniform refusing a bribe, was so nonplussed that he was hauled off to the police station without a word of protest. The general had only wanted to teach the man a lesson, not to have him flogged and sent to Siberia, as seemed certain to happen since it was notoriously difficult to halt any bureaucratic process once it had been set in motion. Fortunately Herzen was able to intervene successfully in person – himself, absurdly enough, confined to Vladimir as a political exile at the time when he performed this kindness (*My Past and Thoughts*, ch. XV).

THE CAUCASUS   To many Russian writers the Caucasus was the most fascinating region of the Empire, and a greater contrast with the Russian plain was hard to imagine. In the narrow sense the name Caucasus applies to the mountain chain of the Great Caucasus, about seven hundred and fifty miles long, running from the Black Sea in the north-west to the Caspian in the south-east and reaching the height of 18,470 feet with Mount Elbrus. More generally the Caucasus denotes a larger area, including some territory (Ciscaucasia) north of the central range and more extensive lands to the south (Transcaucasia), among which are Georgia, Armenia and Azerbaydzhan.

There is probably no area on the face of the globe with a greater diversity of ethnic origins and languages. This applies especially to the mountain peoples, who include among many others the Lezghians of Dagestan; the Chechens in the east; and the Abkhazians and Circassians in the west. Of the two ancient Christian peoples of Caucasia, the Georgians were closer to Russians by religion, since they practised the Orthodox faith – they had been converted to Christianity in the year 318. The Armenians, converted even earlier to Christianity, had their own Armenian Gregorian Church. Many other peoples of the Caucasus, including the Tatars (Azerbaydzhanis) mentioned above among Turkic-speaking peoples, and numerous mountain tribes, were Muslim.

During the first six decades of the century it was possible to campaign in the Caucasus, as did the young Tolstoy, against 'savage' (still independent) mountain tribes on Russia's equivalent of British India's North-West Frontier. At Pyatigorsk in the Northern Caucasus Russia's greatest romantic poet Lermontov met his death in a duel. His novel *A Hero of Our Time* and his poems *The Demon* (1839) and *Mtsyri* (1840) are among the many literary works inspired by this wild and picturesque territory. Pushkin's *Prisoner of the Caucasus* (1822) is also set in the exotic south, as are Tolstoy's posthumous novel *Hadji Murat* and some of his earliest stories.

Like the English Lakes, the Caucasus inspired the country's poets, but the atmosphere was less elegiac, and anything but Wordsworthian. It was neither Little Lucy nor the springs of Dove that one might expect to meet round the bends of Chechnya's mountain tracks so much as a bullet in the neck.

6 The economy

BACKWARDNESS   To many educated Russians the Empire's economic organisation seemed appallingly backward when comparison was made with the advanced industrial countries of the world. While other nations pioneered economic progress Russia still stagnated under serfdom and its aftermath. Technical skill and capital must clearly be acquired if the Empire was to compete. But was this truly desirable? Many believed that it was not, and some – the slavophiles – tended to regard 'progress' on the western model as unsuitable for Russia. This was only a minority view, however, and after the disastrous Crimean War even extreme conservatives became impressed by the urgent need to modernise the economy.

AGRICULTURE   The nineteenth century did not see the full transformation of Russia into a modern industrial state. It was with a mainly agricultural economy on a low level of technical development, and with a largely illiterate, primitive and rural population that the Empire ended the century – as she had begun it. In 1900 agriculture remained, as in 1800, the main branch of the economy, at least in the number of people engaged in it. Even by the early twentieth century some three quarters of the population were still employed in agriculture and the allied pursuits of forestry, fishing and hunting, and it is against this background of a predominant agriculture that the rise of Russian industry must be seen.

Grain was the most important product. In terms of exports, however, flax and hemp exceeded grain in value until overtaken by it in the mid-1840s. The largest crop in the north and centre was rye, grown chiefly for home consumption. But the export trade was increasingly dominated by the expanding production of south Russian wheat, shipped from Black Sea ports, of which Odessa became the most important. In 1856–60 the grain trade accounted for thirty-five per cent of the over-all value of exports, and by the last three decades of the century it had risen even further and came to roughly half (Blum, p. 288; Florinsky, ii, p. 939). Yet these exports formed only a small proportion of the total Russian cereal production, most of which was consumed in Russia itself. Agricultural methods were proverbially inefficient. 'Comparative data collected around the middle of the century revealed that Russian yields were lower than those of any other European nation' (Blum, p. 330). And yet, owing to the vast areas available for cultivation, the production of grain per head of population was greater than that of any other European country. Other crops – sugar beet, potatoes and grapes for wine – acquired importance too, animal husbandry being relatively neglected.

INDUSTRY BEFORE EMANCIPATION Based as it was on serfdom, the Russian economy of the early nineteenth century made an antiquated and bizarre impression. Many factories – for example, the metallurgical works and mines of the Urals – were chiefly manned by forced labour. On the other hand, cotton manufacture, the most rapidly growing branch of Russian industry in the first half of the nineteenth century, depended largely on hired labour. Hired labourers were free in the sense of not being the property of their industrial employer or factory, but it did not follow that they were not serfs. Many had leave of absence from their owners on condition of paying *obrok* (annual money dues). Since textiles were booming while the heavy industry of the Urals stagnated, many Russian employers drew the conclusion sometimes reached by historians later – that forced labour was unproductive. So it indeed was, but this was only one of the factors retarding Russia's economic growth by comparison with that achieved elsewhere. Others included poor communications over much greater distances. Commodities could multiply many times in price by the time they had been hauled hundreds or thousands of miles by sledge, boat and rail.

In Russia before 1861 most factory workers were peasants and serfs. They enjoyed much variety in their status and conditions of work. Some worked for no pay on *barshchina* (*corvée*) in factories owned by their masters – distilleries, sugar-beet mills and other 'agricultural' industries in the early years of the century belonging mainly to members of the gentry. Other serfs, notably from the overpopulated and agriculturally poor regions, were, as indicated above, permitted by their owners to hire themselves out as 'free' labour on condition of paying *obrok*. Others again were 'possessional' serfs attached to a factory and enjoying 'limited serf status', while members of all categories might be skilled or unskilled, part-time or full-time. One surprising feature is that an energetic serf could, with his owner's connivance, become an industrialist and even a millionaire, himself controlling, if not legally possessing, serfs of his own and employing hired labourers.

COTTAGE INDUSTRY   An important branch of the economy, rapidly expanding in the early nineteenth century, was cottage industry, whereby work was contracted out to peasants in their own homes. The products might be commissioned by factories, hawked by pedlars, or sold at one of the great fairs – those of Nizhny Novgorod and of Irbit in western Siberia being the most celebrated. The products of the agriculturally poor northern and central provinces tended to find their way, by an appropriate division of labour, to the richer agricultural land of south Russia, which in turn produced a surplus of grain to feed the poorer provinces. Industrial progress did not kill the cottage industries, and some seven or eight million persons were so employed in the early twentieth century, earning about 500 million roubles a year (Kovalevsky, p. 512).

INDUSTRIALISATION   Even before 1861 the economy was by no means stagnant, and the value of exports and imports almost tripled between 1826 and 1860. Then, after emancipation, economic development proceeded at a new pace, reaching a particularly high rate of growth in the 1890s. The old-fashioned merchant increasingly gave way to the businessman, industrialist and technician, while more antiquated aspects of the economy were yielding to such features of developed capitalism as joint stock companies, stock exchanges and private banks. An industrial labour force of about two hundred thousand in 1800 (exact statistics are not available) had multiplied about fourfold by 1860, and has been calculated at roughly three million all told for the year 1900 (Seton-Watson, p. 123). Serf workmen had given way to a growing industrial proletariat and the themes of labour legislation, trade unions and strikes begin to be heard.

Internal revenue was mainly raised by indirect taxation, and excise duty on spirits – merging at the end of the century into a state monopoly of spirits – provided the most productive single item. As a poor country Russia needed foreign credit to industrialise, and became the largest borrower in Europe. At first these funds were chiefly directed to building railways. Then heavy industry received an impetus from the discovery of iron ore at Krivoy Rog in south Russia and from the development of coalmining in the Donets Basin two hundred miles to the east. When these two centres were connected by railway in 1884, south Russian industry was thoroughly launched. It in turn fed railway development and also produced armaments, leaving the original heavy industrial centre of the Urals far behind. The main industrial centre in the Donets Basin was founded in 1869 as Yuzovka (now Donetsk) after the Welshman John Hughes, head of the New Russia Metallurgical Company, which set up a plant there. Important industrial development also took place in the Caucasus with the exploitation of the oil wells at Baku, and of the less productive field at Grozny. During the four years 1898 to 1901 Russia was, amazingly, producing more oil than the rest of the world put together.

Sergey Witte, minister of finance from 1892 to 1903, played a crucial part in the industrialisation drive. He helped economic development by monetary reform, by encouraging the building of railways, by attracting foreign loans and investments, and also by his policy of tariff protection and of government subsidies and guarantees to Russian industry.

Industrialising late and rapidly on the basis of foreign experience, Russia often had larger and more modern factories than those of western European industrial countries. But alongside these enterprises were others extremely primitive. In some important spheres – the electrical and chemical industries, the production of machine-tools – the economy remained particularly weak. By the time of the first Russian revolution, in 1905, it had attained a stature which seemed gigantic if compared with that of the pre-emancipation years. Yet when compared with that of Britain, Germany or the United States, the economy still seemed backward – enormous in potential, but mediocre in realisation.

7 Emperors

THE AUTOCRACY   Imperial Russia was an autocracy and its principle of government was, accordingly, that of absolute power exercised by the monarch. From 1613 until the abdication of Nicholas II and end of the monarchy in February 1917, Russia's rulers came from the house of Romanov. From 1721 they held the official title of Emperor (or Empress) of All Russia, first assumed by Peter the Great, but the older title of Tsar, ultimately deriving from Latin *Caesar*, also continued to be used.

The Tsar ruled through his Personal Chancery and through ministers whom he was free to appoint and dismiss at will, and whose power, great or small, depended solely on their standing with him. The ministries and other governmental bodies (the Senate, the Committee of Ministers, the Council of State, the Council of Ministers) are described below, pp. 132–3, as is also the Holy Synod, responsible for church affairs (pp. 102–3). Broadly speaking, none of these institutions enjoyed independence or exercised initiative except in so far as the Tsar periodically heeded their advice, and except for the Senate's function as a court of appeal.

The profession of Tsar was yet more hazardous than that of writer. Three of the last six Tsars met violent deaths, those of Paul (in 1801) and Nicholas II (in 1918) being outside our period. The assassination of Alexander II by revolutionary terrorists in 1881 crowned a long series of earlier attempts on his life, besides which there were also rumours, not wholly discounted by historians, that Nicholas I's death in 1855 was due to suicide by poison. Alexander III died naturally, but there had also been a plot to murder him, that of 1887 which led to the execution of Alexander Ulyanov, elder brother of Lenin. In contrast with the lives of relatives prematurely cut short, Alexander I was rumoured to have lived on as a hermit

under the alias Fyodor Kuzmich for nearly forty years after his
official death in 1825.

One major aim of Russian nineteenth-century liberalism was a
constitution restricting the Tsar's absolute powers. After the
revolution of 1905 this was achieved at least nominally, through concessions extracted from Nicholas II – who did not, however, give
up the title of autocrat. But in the period considered here autocratic
power was not limited.

Three and a half reigns are involved, those of: Nicholas I: 1825–
55; Alexander II: 1855–81; Alexander III: 1881–94; Nicholas II:
1894–1917 (the last thirteen years being outside our period).

Nicholas I and Alexander III were determined, strong-minded
defenders of the autocratic principle, while Alexander II and
Nicholas II were less harsh and uncompromising, and the quartet
accordingly illustrates a tendency for severe and relatively mild Russian rulers to alternate. Alexander II, sometimes called the Tsar-
Liberator, is associated with the many reforms of the 1860s and
1870s, including the emancipation of the serfs, and Nicholas II
granted some constitutional limitations to absolute power, as
mentioned above. But neither would have wished to be remembered
as a liberal. Each was committed to the autocratic principle, and
it happens that each took pains to make this plain in statements
issued shortly after his accession to the throne. The nineteenth century was, therefore, not a period when phases of freedom alternated
with phases of oppression, but one of fluctuating oppression, which
was never – even at its worst – remotely comparable in scope to that
practised by the more oppressive totalitarian states of the twentieth
century.

NICHOLAS I   Conditions were most severe under Nicholas I. The
event which began his reign – the unsuccessful Decembrist revolt
in St Petersburg in 1825 – helped to set him and his successors on
this course, and from 1825 until the abdication of the last Tsar in
1917 fear of revolution haunted Russia's autocrats. Hence the tendency for Russia to support the monarchic principle in Europe and
to oppose popular representation at home and abroad. This attitude
caused imperial Russia to be identified with nineteenth-century
political reaction and to become engaged for example in the suppression of Hungarian revolution in 1849. Hence also the tendency of
nineteenth-century Russia to veer between rigorous repression and

attempts to turn back the revolutionary tide through reforms which on the whole did too little and came too late.

Such vacillations played no great part in Nicholas I's reign. Even then the idea of reform, including the abolition of serfdom, was reviewed in secret governmental committees, but no effective measures were taken. Impulses towards oppression were received through disturbances within the Empire (the Polish revolt of 1830–1) and outside (the European revolutions of 1830 and 1848–9).

A notable innovation of Nicholas I was the establishment, as part of His Majesty's own Chancery, of the so-called Third Section, a special police organisation including a network of secret agents and a uniformed gendarmerie. The first head of the Third Section, from 1826 to 1844, was Count Benckendorff, one of the most powerful figures in the country, responsible to no one save the Emperor himself, and charged, among other duties, with the regimenting of Pushkin. Like Benckendorff himself, many of Nicholas I's other administrators were generals, and the reign has been described as a quasi-military dictatorship by the Tsar.

Nicholas I's policy is aptly summed up in the slogan Orthodoxy, Autocracy and Nationalism, invented by his Minister of Education, S.S. Uvarov. The last of these three terms, in Russian *narodnost*, is the most elusive, but was once eloquently illustrated by Benckendorff in a message addressed to Chaadayev, famous for his disparagement of Russian historical achievement: 'Russia's past is admirable; her present more than magnificent; as to her future, it is beyond the grasp of the most daring imagination; this is the point of view ... from which Russian history must be conceived and written.' Quoting this, the historian Florinsky comments: 'This statement of the Baltic–German nobleman was appropriately delivered in French' (Florinsky, ii, p. 799). He might have added that Benckendorff's master, himself the supreme champion of Russian nationalism, was arguably not a Russian at all – the later Romanovs were overwhelmingly German by descent.

As well as suppressing the Polish rebellion of 1830–1 and the Hungarian rebellion, in 1849 – both episodes involving large-scale Russian troop movements – Nicholas I also fought three external wars. The first, against Persia in 1826–8, ended with the Treaty of Turkmanchay whereby Russia gained the provinces of Nakhichevan and Erivan. The second, against Turkey in 1828–9, ended with the Treaty of Adrianople whereby Russia made further territorial gains, on the Black Sea coast. The third was the Crimean War of 1853-6, fought against Britain, France and Turkey, and ending in a Russian defeat which the Tsar did not live to witness.

Though Nicholas I began his reign by hanging a poet, and though his last eight years (1848-55) were those of the severest oppression in nineteenth-century Russia, literature flourished during this period. The Russia of Nicholas I was also a period of intense intellectual activity in general, when philosophy, social problems and politics were eagerly discussed, at some risk. But the 'conspiracies' unearthed by Nicholas's police were unimpressive. The two most important both had significant literary associations: the case of the Kiev Brotherhood of Cyril and Methodius, founded in 1846, members of which, including the Ukrainian poet Shevchenko, were arrested in the following year; and the case of the Petrashevsky group, arrested in 1849, in which Dostoyevsky and the poet A.N. Pleshcheyev were implicated.

Military defeat tended to hasten reform in Russia. Such was the effect of Russian reverses in the Crimean War and, later, in the Russo-Japanese War of 1904-5. Each of these operations laid bare such incompetence in the workings of imperial Russia that Russians of all shades of opinion tended to feel that the time had come for a change. Coinciding with the death of Nicholas I, defeat in the Crimea thus helped to create a new atmosphere and to usher in the era of reform presided over by Alexander II.

ALEXANDER II How effective indeed were the 'great reforms' of Alexander II? This is still a matter for dispute and it is generally agreed that the most far-reaching, the emancipation of the serfs in 1861, was no unqualified success. Yet 1861 remains the most important single date in nineteenth-century Russian history. Through emancipation the peasants, the most numerous social class in the community, were raised from a level of near-slavery and became free, or at least freer men. But the main benefits of emancipation were moral rather than social or economic. No longer owned by individual landowners, the serfs remained economically dependent and socially inferior after liberation. They were also placed in a form of bondage to their own village communes, where such existed – as in most parts of Great Russia. This put severe limitations on their newly granted freedom. Emancipation was accompanied by widespread peasant disturbances, since many ex-serfs felt cheated and expected a second, real emancipation whereby all the land would be allotted to them and the landowners would be expelled.

The other reforms included the overhaul of judicial procedure, including the establishment of trial by jury. A new system of local government was instituted with the introduction of provincial and district zemstvos (rural councils) and also of municipal councils. Other important reforms removed restrictions on schools and universities. Still others turned the army into less of a penal institution, brought in a fairer conscription system and made military punishments less harsh. The impact of individual reforms will be discussed more fully in later chapters.

Even under Alexander II untoward events continued to activate the machinery of oppression, though they did not deter the Tsar from his determination to enact reforms. Besides peasant disturbances they included a succession of mysterious fires which broke out in St Petersburg in 1862, being widely attributed to revolutionary arsonists. There was also the Polish insurrection of 1863, which once more brought a large Russian army into Poland, and above all the attempt by a former student, Dmitry Karakozov, to assassinate the Tsar in 1866. In the 1870s the atmosphere became still more strained as intellectuals, mainly students, upset authority by taking part in the movement known as 'going to the people' – invading the Russian villages to educate and agitate the peasantry. The movement was suppressed by the government, and was succeeded by the campaign of conspiratorial terrorism which culminated in the assassination of Alexander II in 1881.

In addition to large territorial gains made in Central Asia and the Far East, Alexander II's reign also saw the defeat of Turkey in the war of 1877–8, which ended with the Treaty of San Stefano. By opposing Turkey, Russia emerged as the champion of the Balkan Slavs, and the episode much encouraged extreme Russian nationalism, which flourished on an official level in the next reign.

ALEXANDER III   As a tactical manœuvre the assassination of Alexander II was a failure from the assassins' point of view, since it led to the replacement of a relatively easy-going sovereign by another of tougher fibre. The revolutionary movement lost momentum in the 1880s under the new Tsar, Alexander III, who seemed in many ways a throw-back to his grandfather, Nicholas I. An arch-conservative, he in effect reinstated the slogan Orthodoxy, Auto-

cracy and Nationalism. Religious and ethnic minorities were persecuted, including the Jews – the 1880s being, as already noted, a time
of pogroms, as also of the imposition of a quota for the admission
of Jews to high schools and universities.

A series of measures, some-
times termed counter-reforms, included the imposition of new restrictions on the peasantry, especially by the appointment from
among the gentry of newly instituted officials called land captains
(*zemskiye nachalniki*) with wide powers. Other measures watered
down Alexander II's legal and educational reforms.

In imposing such measures, Alexander III was encouraged by one
of his closest advisers, Konstantin Pobedonostsev, who held the post
of chief procurator of the Holy Synod of the Russian Orthodox
Church from 1880 to 1905 and had been the Tsar's own tutor, as
he also was of the Tsarevich, the future Nicholas II. Pobedonostsev, one of the most powerful men of his age, is portrayed as
'Toporov' in Tolstoy's *Resurrection*. He was only the most influential among a group of ultra-conservative advisers, including such
administrators as Count D.A. Tolstoy, minister of education and
later of internal affairs, and I.N. Durnovo, his successor in the latter
post. There were also journalists, notably M.N. Katkov, who supported and encouraged the Tsar in the successful defence of his
absolute power. Another pillar of autocracy was Dostoyevsky, in
his later years an associate of Katkov and Pobedonostsev.

The great famine of 1891–2 and the ensuing cholera epidemic
were important episodes of Alexander III's reign. Like other dis-
asters of the century, they indirectly encouraged liberal forces, since
the government could not deal with the crisis and felt obliged to
permit the zemstvos and other non-governmental bodies to help
with relief. Tolstoy and Chekhov both took part; Tolstoy helping
to organise a large chain of soup-kitchens for the starving peasants,
and Chekhov, a qualified doctor, directing anti-cholera precautions
in an area of twenty-five villages.

NICHOLAS II   Another calamity, occurring on 18 May 1896 during
the celebration of Nicholas II's coronation, seems in retrospect to
cast an aura of impending doom over the ill-starred reign of Russia's
last autocrat. This was the death of over a thousand people
assembled on the Khodynka Field near Moscow, in a mass stampede
which took place as the result of negligence by the authorities, just
as they were about to receive traditional presents from the Tsar.

A short story by Tolstoy, based on the incident, was published posthumously (*Khodynka*, 1912). On the same evening the Tsar and Tsaritsa tactlessly attended a ball given by the French ambassador, and the episode as a whole seems to set the scene almost too aptly for the twilight of the Romanovs.

Nicholas II did not intend to be the last of Russia's autocrats, seeing himself rather as a defender of absolutism, but he was weaker than his father – a family man, more at ease playing with children and dogs than attempting to arbitrate an Empire's destiny. His policy in appointing and dismissing ministers was erratic. He was easily influenced by unbalanced or unscrupulous advisers and court favourites, the most notorious being Rasputin, whose sway comes outside our period. Nicholas clung tenaciously to supreme power, but by the late 1890s Russia seemed to be acquiring a political and economic momentum of her own. There was a new spirit of independence which even a less weak-willed autocrat might have failed to quell. As Russia advanced, educationally and industrially, the Tsar and his court seemed increasingly anachronistic, and Nicholas himself might have been designed by nature to undermine the system which he had set himself to maintain. That a ruler so out of touch with the realities of his realm could remain in power for twenty-three years, which included two catastrophic major wars, argues more stability in the Russian monarchy as an institution than historians have sometimes allowed.

The most crucial events of Nicholas II's reign fall outside our period, being: the Russo-Japanese War of 1904–5; the first Russian revolution, that of 1905; and above all the First World War, which weakened the structure of imperial Russia until the monarchy collapsed with the last Emperor's abdication at the time of the February revolution of 1917.

Part Three
THE SOCIAL SETTING

8 The 'estates'

The Empire's population, both Russian and non-Russian, fell into various social categories according to a complicated system. In the first instance the vast majority of the inhabitants were classified as native subjects. These comprised the entire population (including non-Russians) except for three relatively small groups: foreign nationals resident in Russia; the inhabitants of Finland; and certain peoples officially termed those 'of other race' (*inorodtsy*) – they included Jews and members of various primitive tribes.

Among the above the inhabitants of Finland were further subdivided into social classes according to a separate system. But what of the categories into which the native subjects of the Empire, and also the Jews, were subdivided? To one or other of these groups (*sosloviya* or *sostoyaniya*), here termed 'estates', every individual was obliged at least in theory to belong. Each estate had its own special status in law and its own peculiar advantages or obligations.

There was thus no general category of Russian citizen. There were instead the estates of the gentry (hereditary and individual), clergy and peasantry. There were also several groups into which 'town-dwellers' were divided, those of honorary citizens (hereditary and individual); merchants; craftsmen; burghers (*meshchane*). As a further complication, however, only about half of the country's urban residents were members of town-dwellers' estates, the remainder belonging to other categories – chiefly the peasantry. The Cossacks too rated as an estate, being divided into gentry and ordinary Cossacks. As is shown by the existence of a Cossack gentry, members of which belonged in a sense to two estates, the borderline between these groups was not precise, and membership of one estate need not exclude membership of another. It was also customary to speak of members of the armed forces as belonging to the military estates, though many officers were of course also members of the gentry. Civil servants were said to form an estate, though all of them above a certain grade also belonged to the gentry as well.

Closer examination only confirms the unsystematic pattern presented by the Empire's social strata. In certain groups children automatically inherited the social status of their parents, as was the case with the hereditary gentry, hereditary honorary citizens, burghers and peasants. In other groups – those of the merchants, individual gentry and individual honorary citizens – status was not so transmitted. Most groups possessed a corporate organisation – the assemblies of the gentry; the merchants' guilds; the craft corporations; the burghers' and peasants' communes. But the honorary citizens had no such organisation. Corporate organisations might exist below and up to the level of provinces, as they did in the case of the gentry. In one case there was overall control over a whole estate on an all-Russian level, since the whole clergy came under the supervision of the Holy Synod.

The legal position of the estates changed during the course of the century and the situation became more fluid. At one time the gentry and clergy were called 'privileged' because their members enjoyed three advantages: freedom from conscription, from corporal punishment and from personal taxation. Hence the other estates were sometimes termed 'unprivileged' or 'taxed'. With the restrictions on corporal punishment enacted in 1863, the introduction of universal liability to conscription in 1874 and the abolition of the poll-tax by 1887, the gap between privileged and unprivileged citizens was considerably reduced. However, the status of gentleman continued to confer certain advantages compared with membership of the other estates.

For an individual to move from one estate to another was by no means uncommon. The attainment of sufficiently high military or civil rank automatically conferred entry to the gentry, and the possession of sufficient funds made it possible for traders to register as merchants. Conversely, bankruptcy could reduce a merchant to the level of a mere burgher, as happened to Chekhov's father, an unsuccessful grocer.

The relative size of the groups may be judged by the following figures showing the membership of the main estates or groups of estates as a percentage of the population at the end of the nineteenth century (from Kovalevsky, p. 67):

Peasants	81·5 per cent
'Town-dwellers'	9 per cent
Military estates	6·5 per cent
Gentry	just over 1 per cent
Clergy	just under 1 per cent

The position of individual social groups is discussed in greater detail below.

9 Peasants

GENERAL SITUATION The estate of the peasantry accounted for an overwhelming majority of the Empire's inhabitants, about four out of every five persons – in many ways a class apart, as they have remained, to some extent, even in the late twentieth century. In the nineteenth century peasants spoke, as they speak today, a Russian more earthy and vivid than that of the intellectual, but surprisingly uniform within the Great Russian area if comparison is made with the variety of dialects in such countries as Germany and Italy. Most peasants were illiterate: even as late as 1897 census data showed that only twenty-two per cent of the rural population between the ages of nine and forty-nine could read and write (Utechin, *Encyclopaedia*, p. 225).

The peasants were often said to carry the Empire on their backs. Even after emancipation they were still far from enjoying the freedom and privileges available to more fortunate sections of the community, and they bore an excessive share of the tax burden. Their housing, clothing and food were of miserable quality. They were generally devoted to the Tsar – in popular mythology a benevolent figure misled by the evil officials and landowners who stood between him and his humbler subjects.

The peasants were given to extremes of kindness and cruelty. They were prone to riot, loot the local manor-house, murder the squire and his family and 'let loose the red cock' by setting fire to his property. As for violence between peasants, the beating of wives and children was distressingly prevalent, but peasants were also regular church-goers, and kept the strict prescribed fasts. Bullied and patronised in turn by the privileged classes of Russia, to whom they seemed a sinister enigma, but also the repository of some mysterious virtue defying analysis, they were designated by the potent emotional word *narod*, which can also mean 'people' or 'nation'.

They also had the habit of calling themselves 'dark people' (*tyom-nyye lyudi*).

SOME PEASANTS IN LITERATURE   Russian literature has much to say about peasant life, one of the best-known works concerned being Gogol's *Dead Souls*. Peasant characters play small part in it, but an eloquent comment on serfdom is conveyed by the hero's attempt to buy up and mortgage 'dead souls' – male serfs who had expired since the previous census, but were subject to tax until the next one. In the late 1840s the emerging realist movement generated several works about the Russian peasantry, of which Turgenev's *Sportsman's Sketches* are the best known. Grigorovich's stories *The Village* and *Poor Anton* were other influential portrayals of serfs. Among later descriptions of the peasant, those of Tolstoy and Chekhov are major contributions from fiction-writers of the front rank, Chekhov's story *Peasants* (1897) containing an especially good short description of Russian village life. Populist writers of the late nineteenth century, including Gleb Uspensky and Alexander Ertel, also treated the theme (see below, p. 174). Nor was the peasant neglected in poetry, Aleksey Koltsov, Ivan Nikitin and – in his very different way – Nekrasov being among those who used peasant idiom in verse. Nekrasov's long narrative poem *Who Can Be Happy in Russia?* contains lively passages, but its mournful title and the miseries which it describes set the tone for much of Russian peasant literature. This tends to be sad, but so too was the average peasant's life.

SERFS   There were about fifty million peasants in all at the time of emancipation. Of these slightly less than half were serfs – they belonged, that is, to individual landowning masters. The word serf is also sometimes loosely but incorrectly applied to the large class of state peasants who lived on property owned and administered by the state, and who outnumbered the serfs proper at the time of emancipation (Blum, pp. 476–7). There were other categories too, including the 'appanage' peasants who lived on properties belonging to the imperial court. It was the serfs proper who suffered the severest conditions on the whole – especially those who were taken into the squire's house as domestic servants (*dvorovyye lyudi*) – always under the master's eye and eventually emancipated without land. This did not prevent some of them from hankering, like the

aged manservant Firs in Chekhov's *Cherry Orchard*, after the good
old days before the Troubles – Firs's word for the emancipation.

Some of the serfs' troubles arose from the system termed *barshchina* (*corvée*), whereby two or three days' unpaid labour a week was
due to the squire, and more might easily be exacted. Then again,
despite feeble attempts by the government to limit the worst abuses
of the serf system, landowners could in practice do as they liked
with their serfs – mortgage them, separate them from their families,
lose them at cards, consign them to the army for twenty-five years
or have them flogged. A kind-hearted landlord might grant his
peasants relief by changing the *barshchina* system for that of an
annual money-due (*obrok*), as did Eugene Onegin in Pushkin's
verse novel, who (to give a somewhat unpoetical translation) 'substi-
tuted an easy *obrok* for the yoke of burdensome *barshchina*' on his
newly inherited estate. As the *obrok* system reminds us, serfs were
by no means bonded to the soil. Provided that they paid the required
dues, they were permitted, indeed encouraged, to seek employment
where they could find it, perhaps many hundreds of miles from
home. They might, as shown above, become part-time or full-time
factory workers, and it was through this system that a large proportion of the urban population of Russia consisted of peasants (for
the landlord–serf relationship, see further pp. 98–100 below).

DWELLINGS   Both before and after emancipation Russian villages,
and the peasant huts of which they were largely composed, made
a melancholy impression. This was partly due to the uniformity of
the buildings and to the layout of the villages, especially in Great
Russia, with which we are chiefly concerned. It was not normal,
as in many countries, to have isolated peasant holdings. Huts were
usually set close together, each standing on its oblong plot. A typical
small village thus consisted of two rows of huts separated by the
'road' – a broad, unpaved strip of mud, slush, dust or snow, according to the weather. Larger villages were diversified by side-roads
running at right angles, and visual relief might be supplied by the
village church, especially if it had brightly painted onion-domes.

Within a given area all villages tended to look alike, though there
were variations in style from one part of the country to another.
Wood was the main building material. The walls were of logs laid
horizontally on top of one another, the cracks being stuffed with
moss or tow, and the frames of windows and doorways often being

elaborately carved. The size of huts varied according to the avail-
ability of manpower and timber. They tended to be larger in northern villages, where wood was abundantly available. Here they might
rise to two storeys, apart from which they would have a fairly roomy
'cellar' (*podklet*) obtained by setting the living-room floor five to
ten feet above the ground at the level between the sixth and tenth
beam up. Hence the characteristic height of the living-room windows in a Russian hut when viewed from street level. The cellar
was used for hens, for the young of domestic animals and for storage.
Further to the south, shortage of timber made it necessary to
economise on the height of the cellar and on size generally. It also
brought an important structural variation – the use of straw thatch
instead of wood as roofing material.

Peasants usually built their own homes, often being as adept with
their axes as they were with scythe and sickle. Three men working
hard could construct a typical hut in a few weeks, and the modest
outbuildings required even less time. As this illustrates, the peasants
tended to be economically self-sufficient, the women being as skilled
with loom and spindle as the men with their axes. It was largely
a subsistence economy. Peasants made their own dwellings, clothes
and agricultural gear, and used little money – though the use of
money was on the increase.

The heart of the peasant homestead was the heated living-room.
It served as dining-room, kitchen and bedroom combined for the
whole family, which might include three or even four generations.
The most important inanimate object was a huge stove of brick or
rammed clay, occupying a sixth or more of the total area. By the
end of the century it was customary to equip stoves with chimneys,
but in earlier huts so-called 'black' heating was the rule: the stove
spouted its smoke straight into the living-room, an ordeal to the
uninitiated. But the Russian peasant was inured to this, having been
rocked and (one is tempted to add) kippered in a cradle near the
ceiling, where smoke was thickest, in his earliest years.

As a visitor entered a typical living-room the stove might be on
the right of the door as he went in, and he would find himself facing
the wall which gave on to the street and had three small windows,
probably not more than two feet high and one foot wide. Another
similar window, to the left, might look out on the yard. On the left
corner (the so-called 'red' or 'front' corner) of the wall facing the
road there would be a shelf or case containing an icon with a lamp

burning in front of it, and every visitor would be expected to face this and cross himself on entering the room.

Beds and chairs were usually dispensed with, the functions of both being fulfilled by wooden benches running along the walls. Peasants usually slept in or under their daytime clothes. In addition to the benches a structure known as the *polati* – removable boards set on posts at about the height of the top of the stove and usually placed against the wall facing the windows – provided, together with the stove itself, a warm sleeping-platform. This eminence was also convenient for stowing dotards and children, and as a vantage-point from which they could watch domestic dramas unfold below them. A crude table, a cupboard containing half a dozen bowls, wooden spoons, a few knives, dishes, pots and other utensils, a washing-tub – these would almost complete the simple inventory, together with pictures, cut out of magazines and pasted on the wall. They might portray the Russian Imperial Family, biblical scenes, the battles of Inkerman and Alma, St George and the Dragon or episodes from Russian folk-lore. One important and much-prized item might also be found: the samovar for boiling water to make tea, a favourite peasant drink and a great luxury.

In a country where the neglectful froze to death in winter the stove was a vital item, providing warmth, together with bread-baking and other cooking facilities. It might also be possible to take a steam-bath inside the huge oven, as was common in the south. In the north, where timber was plentiful and the influence of the Finnish sauna may be suspected, a peasant household often had its own bath-house – a small, crude hut with a stove, set away from the main hut. The peasants' steam-bath on Saturday nights was an important part of their weekly ritual, and in winter many of them enjoyed a roll in the snow after steaming themselves and lashing themselves with birch switches.

Matches were luxuries, and peasants who lacked them would bank up the stove at night and blow on it to revive it in the morning. Clumsily managed stoves might disgorge poisonous fumes (*ugar*), whence the idiom 'to thrash around like an *ugorely*' (one who has been subjected to carbon monoxide fumes from a Russian stove). As for lighting, paraffin lamps too were a luxury, at least until late in the century, and when they were unavailable burning strips of wood (*luchiny*) were set on a special stand to provide a meagre, smoky glow.

So much for the typical living-room. For purposes of heat conservation it did not open directly on the outside world, but was approached through an entrance-lobby, the *seni*. On the other side of this from the living-room might be a storeroom (*klet*) – unheated, but used as an overflow living-room in summer. To enter his yard from the main living-room the peasant might turn right after stepping into the lobby and go out through a porch. He might then find, on his right, a high wooden fence, continuing the line of the front of the hut, with its small door and large gate giving on to the road. Opposite him might be his carts, sledges, ploughs and other impedimenta, stowed in the open under the overhanging roof of the shed which housed any horses, cows and sheep. There might be a pig-sty adjoining it, and round at the back might be the grain-store, threshing-barn and kitchen-garden.

Such, with many local variations, were the dwellings built by Russian peasants where timber was available. Wood supplied shelter and fuel. But in the treeless steppe of the south, including the Ukraine, huts were heated with dried dung and were made of rammed clay or wattle. They were whitewashed, stood in their own gardens, and were scattered about in disregard of the rectilinear principles practised in the forests. They were also normally known by a different name (*khata* instead of *izba*) and might present a more cheerful spectacle, at least in the Ukraine. But the huts of southern Great Russia were particularly wretched.

The miseries of the peasantry were increased by the constant danger of fire, and the Russian language even has a special word – *pogorelets* – to describe someone rendered homeless and destitute by having his hut burnt down. Fire also inspired a common Russian proverb: 'My hut's on the end' (i.e. at the opposite end of the village to the fire), the equivalent of the English 'I'm all right, Jack'. Chekhov's *Peasants* contains a good short description of a fire which occurred through carelessness with a samovar and was fortunately extinguished, before much damage had been caused, by a young squire of the locality, helped by women hauling water from the river and surrounded by the less helpful drunken muzhiks who staggered out of the village inn.

MARRIAGE The peasants' attitude to their womenfolk was rarely chivalrous or sentimental. A wife, like a horse, was a necessary beast of burden and marriages were commonly planned with an eye to economic advantage, being arranged by the young people's parents. However, love matches – sometimes by elopement followed by a plea for the parents' forgiveness – were by no means unknown, and they became more common towards the end of the period. Peasants usually married young, the girls at sixteen to eighteen years and the men a year or two later.

Peasant marriage was associated with traditional rituals so complex – and with so many local variations – that we cannot describe them in detail. They often began with the ceremony of matchmaking, whereby a team of negotiators (perhaps consisting of the young man's uncle or elder brother with wives, godparents and other interested parties) set out at night – to avoid detection – for the home of some marriageable girl. On receiving a favourable response from her parents they would arrange a further meeting to discuss the dowry and the financial contribution to be made by the groom's family to the wedding. In some areas this discussion was called 'the little booze-up' (*maly zapoy*). It was followed after an appropriate interval by 'the big booze-up', in effect a betrothal ceremony after which neither side could honourably withdraw.

On the wedding eve bride and groom held separate farewell parties for their friends of the same sex. The bride also took a steambath on that day or on the wedding day itself, when she was dressed by her unmarried female friends. The groom went in procession with his best man and various assistants to the bride's home, where a number of ceremonies might be performed, including the symbolic purchase of the bride. After the wedding ceremony bride and groom were conducted to the nuptial couch by the chief female matchmaker (*svakha*) and best man (*druzhka*), and it was the bride's first duty to remove her husband's boots as a sign of submissiveness. On the following morning the matchmaker and best man would waken the couple and display the bride's smock in a condition reputedly offering proof of her virginity before marriage.

It was not uncommon for wedding festivities to last six days, not to mention various follow-up celebrations spread over the ensuing weeks and months. By the end of the century, however. these practices were being generally simplified and curtailed.

CHILDREN A high birth rate and a high rate of infant mortality were characteristic of peasant families, and Marya (in Chekhov's *Peasants*) who 'had thirteen children, of whom only six had lived' was therefore by no means exceptional. Though Russian peasant women are renowned for giving birth in the fields at harvest time, babies were more commonly delivered by a peasant midwife (*povitukha*) on the shelf in the family bath-hut – a small shack separate from the main peasant homestead, as described above. The practice was thought to protect the hut proper from the pollution supposedly associated with childbirth, and also to shield the new-born infant from the evil eye. The mother might well be working in the fields a week later. Christening usually followed a day or two after birth. The child was commonly slung from the ceiling of the hut in a cradle and was breast-fed up to the age of a year or eighteen months. The practice of imprisoning infants in tight swaddling clothes, from which they are periodically released for a delicious feed and romp, has been invoked as an explanation of the national character – allegedly prone to switch between extremes of gloom and gaiety, sloth and wild activity. Peasant children led a hard life. They were often beaten, were expected to defer to their elders and were required to undertake family chores (weaving for the girls, farm-work for the boys) as soon as they were able. In certain areas they might be despatched to a town at the age of twelve, the girls as domestic servants, the boys as apprentice waiters, cobblers, bakers and so on.

FUNERALS The body of a dead peasant was laid out on a bench in the 'red' corner (that containing the icon) of his hut, with his head towards the icon. The deceased was carried to the funeral in an open coffin, and it was customary to hold a 'wake' (*pominki*) after the ceremony – not always as uproarious an affair as that which crowns the obsequies of Marmeladov in Dostoyevsky's *Crime and Punishment*, nor yet necessarily as poignant as that which commemorates Lipa's murdered infant in Chekhov's *In the Hollow*.

DRINKING HABITS The typical village inn was one more hut, perhaps somewhat larger than its neighbours, and would even house the usual icon with a lamp burning in front of it. 'The floor is dirty', according to one description of a typical inn, dated 1898, 'and so are both walls and tables. Even dirtier are the red cotton tablecloths with which they are covered in some places. The lamp, which dimly lights the pub, is dirty, the glasses and crockery are dirty. There is dust everywhere' (Isayev, p. 40). But the customers are not fussy, the same observer points out, conveying a positively idyllic picture of the village inn. Humble it might be with its bar at one end of the room, holding a few bottles of vodka, half a dozen of beer, some salted gherkins and hunks of rye bread on small plates. But it was the social hub of the village, serving as a club where gossip could be exchanged or commercial deals concluded in congenial surroundings, and where old soldiers could relive the Turkish campaign of 1877–8 and their memories of the siege of Plevna. It also served as a reading-room and as a place where some village 'scholar' might regale his illiterate fellow-peasants with extracts from a tattered newspaper. Local politics too were discussed – the election of a new village elder, the eccentricities of the parish priest, the misdoings of the local tax inspector.

Disappointingly – at least to those who would conceive the village inn as a den of vice – the favourite drink was tea, served by the pot or, for a large group of customers, brewed from the samovar. It was customary to drink glass after glass of tea, growing red in the face until according to Russian idiom it brought out the 'seventh sweat'. For this reason it was sometimes possible to order 'tea, sugar and a towel'.

By no means did the peasant scorn alcohol. Surprisingly, though, in view of his reputation as a heavy drinker, the *per capita* consumption of alcohol throughout the largely peasant Empire was strikingly low compared with that of France, Britain, Germany and Denmark (Schlesinger, p. 14; Bruford, p. 46). These figures do not, however, allow for the common practice of brewing *samogon* ('hooch' or poteen). It must also be added that the Russian peasant was a selective drinker who tended to confine his potations to special occasions. These were plentiful indeed. 'According to an established custom, sanctified by time and by tradition (as is claimed in an official report of 1903) not one event in the social life of the community (such, for example, as the cutting of the hay, or the celebration of the local saint's day), can be gotten through without the drinking of *vodka*; and in just the same way *vodka* is indispensable on very important occasions in the life of the family: at birth, marriages, funeral-feasts, the leave-taking of recruits, and the like' (quoted in Robinson, p. 259).

It was in no half-hearted, niggling style that the villager tackled his liquor on these occasions, and Chekhov's account (in *Peasants*) admirably conveys the atmosphere:

On Elijah's Day they drank. On the Feast of the Assumption they drank. On Holy Cross Day they drank. The Feast of the Intercession was the parish holiday ... and the villagers seized the chance to drink for three days. They drank their way through fifty roubles of communal funds and then the village had a whip-round for more vodka. The Chikildeyevs killed a sheep on the first day and ate vast helpings of it morning, noon and night, and even then the children got up at night for a bite. Kiryak was terribly drunk on all three days. He drank the cap off his head and the boots off his feet, and beat Marya so hard that she had to be doused with water. Later on everyone felt ashamed and sick.

FESTIVALS   As the above extract illustrates, the peasant reckoned his dates by the Orthodox Church calendar, not by months and days. The following table contains the main fixed festivals celebrated by the peasantry, the dates on which they were held being those of the Julian Calendar (used in Russia until 1918) which, as has been said, lagged behind the Gregorian Calendar (used in western Europe) by twelve days in the nineteenth century and by thirteen days in the twentieth century.

6 January	Epiphany
2 February	*Sreteniye* (The Meeting)
25 March	Annunciation
9 May	St Nicholas's Day (summer)
29 June	St Peter and St Paul's Day
6 August	Transfiguration
15 August	Assumption, Dormition
29 August	The Decapitation of St John the Baptist
8 September	Nativity of the Virgin
14 September	Holy Cross Day
26 September	Death of St John the Apostle
1 October	Intercession of the Virgin
22 October	Our Lady of Kazan
21 November	Presentation of Our Lady
6 December	St Nicholas's Day (winter)
25–27 December	Christmas

Four movable feasts must be added to the above: Easter (the most important of all); Ascension (forty days after Easter); and Whitsun (ten days after Ascension Day), as well as Shrovetide or Carnival preceding Lent.

FASTS Severe fasts were observed on almost half the days of the year, when the consumption of meat, milk, butter and eggs was forbidden. In each week Wednesday (the day on which Judas betrayed Christ), as well as the more familiar Friday, was a fast day, besides which there were also four extended fast periods: St Peter's Fast (lasting five weeks and ending on 29th June, the Day of St Peter and St Paul); the Fast of the Assumption (two weeks before 15th August); and the Christmas Fast (six weeks ending on 24th December). A tendency sometimes noted in Russian peasants – to switch from the extreme of self-indulgence to the extreme of mortification of the flesh – was thus encouraged and sanctified by the Orthodox Church calendar. But, since they were often desperately poor, the element of mortification tended to predominate over that of self-indulgence. With the wealthier classes, especially merchants, the opposite might be the case, but peasants took their fasts seriously, often to the detriment of their health – especially as the fasts of St Peter and of the Assumption occurred when field work was at its height.

DIET The peasantry's diet was simple: mainly black (rye) bread, supplemented by buckwheat gruel, potatoes, cabbage, cucumber and onions. To the luxuries of tea and vodka, mentioned above, must be added the more humdrum national drink – kvass made from fermented black bread. Meat was a rare luxury, and little milk was drunk.

DRESS The poorer peasants' working clothes tended to be simple home-made articles. In summer they might go barefoot or would wear bast shoes (*lapti*), while felt boots (*valenki*) supplied protection against the cold of winter. They wore trousers, linen shirts and various styles of coat or tunic, including the caftan and *poddyovka*. Sheepskin coats were worn in winter, sometimes with an extra large topcoat (*tulup*), also usually of sheepskin and bound round with a coloured cummerbund. This was essential for winter travel, owing to the use of open sleighs. Hence the close association between peasants and the smell of sheepskins in descriptions of winter in literature.

Peasants kept more elaborate clothes in reserve for holidays, when the better-off young men might wear baggy velveteen trousers (*sharovary*). Resplendent in bright shirts made of bought material, village dandies sometimes sported a single silver ear-ring. Great importance was attached to the possession of highly polished top-boots, into which trousers were tucked, and which were so prized that young men sometimes took them off when they had to walk through mud.

Peasants, especially before the emancipation, did not shave their beards. The most characteristic headgear was a felt affair shaped something like a top-hat, and they had fur caps, preferably with ear-flaps, for winter wear.

The clothes of peasant women offered greater variety, but with the same tendency to keep special dresses for holidays. The most characteristic item was the *sarafan*, a sleeveless over-dress. On holidays elaborately embroidered or ornamented clothes might be worn, including the *kokoshnik*, a head-dress adorned with artificial pearls in place of the humble but gaudy kerchief worn on ordinary working days.

PEASANT FARMING   St George's Day (23rd April) was considered the beginning of work in the fields in many parts, and until early June the sowing of spring corn was the chief occupation. The second half of June was devoted to ploughing for winter corn. With the arrival of St Peter and St Paul's Day on 29th June came haymaking – carried out by the village men, using scythes. Reaping was done by sickle in Great Russia, and this work, in which both men and women joined, was reckoned the hardest of all. By tradition Elijah's Day (20th July) marked the beginning and Assumption (15th August) the end of the harvest. With the gathering of the spring-sown corn and the sowing of the winter corn for the following year, the exhausting but short agricultural cycle of under six months was finished. By 1st October, the Feast of the Intercession, the peasant was back in his hut with nothing but the threshing between him and his winter occupations. Depending on age, temperament and resources, these might involve mending and making agricultural implements, work of cottage industry type in his own home, non-agricultural seasonal work in a town – or simply lazing on the stove.

Phenomenally energetic though the peasant might be during his five or six months in the fields, he was not among Europe's more efficient farmers. This was due to causes other than lack of strength and intelligence. Primitive methods and primitive implements were still in use at the end of the century. The traditional light, wheelless plough (*sokha*) was still widely employed, but did not cut deep enough to turn an adequate furrow. The three-field method of cropping (similar to the medieval strip system long generally abandoned in western Europe) was commonly followed. It involved putting one field down to winter corn and another to spring corn, while a third was left fallow, the crops being rotated annually. A peasant household held a narrow strip in each of the three fields, or several strips in each field, the different holdings often being far separated both from each other and from the cultivator's hut, with consequent waste of time on going from one to the other. The narrowness of the strips, sometimes as little as two yards across, precluded cross-ploughing and resulted in land being wasted on providing boundaries.

Individual farmers were discouraged from improving their land by the communal system of tenure whereby, in most of the Great Russian area of European Russia, arable areas were liable to periodical repartition. Owing to the neglect of animal husbandry manure was in short supply, and in any case there was little point in clearing or manuring land when it was liable to be reallocated at the next repartition. Other handicaps included unsuitable soil and climatic conditions – the bogs and infertile lands of central Russia and the insufficient rainfall of the black earth region, immensely fertile though it potentially was. The difficulty of transporting produce, owing to poor communications, was yet another major disadvantage.

We must add the traditional 'go-slow' mentality bred in the peasants by centuries of oppression. Their attitude to the squire, who owned them along with the land before emancipation, was marked by profound suspicion which continued long after the peasants had become free men and had begun to work for the local landowner as paid labourers. Well-meaning landowners might sincerely propose generous innovations to benefit the peasantry, as do Levin in *Anna Karenin*, Nekhlyudov in *Resurrection* and many other Tolstoyan heroes. But the peasants remained stubbornly convinced that these would-be philanthropists were concerned only to cheat and exploit them. Their attitude hampered those landlords who wished to improve farming methods by mechanisation, for the peasants often refused to use the new machinery, and would break it – accidentally or on purpose.

COMMUNES   After emancipation mere removal – even if permanent residence was involved – to a town, did not cause a villager to lose the legal status of peasant. By one of the emancipation's more irksome provisions, peasants belonging to a village commune remained permanently attached to that body, which now took over some of the original serf-owners' claims on individuals.

The commune was known as *obshchestvo* ('society') and sometimes as *obshchina* or *mir*. It is its composition and functions, rather than its highly controversial origins, which concern us here. The village contained a number of households, each normally consisting of a single family inhabiting a single dwelling. A household might include numerous daughters-in-law and grandchildren, though there was a tendency for large families to split up after emancipation. One person, normally the oldest non-senile male, was head of the household, and the governing body of the commune consisted of a meeting of all heads of households. Not all were men, for a widowed woman might attend and speak if she happened to be the head of her household.

The meetings of heads of household usually took place in the open air on holidays or Sundays amid lively discussion by members no less articulate for being mostly illiterate, and by a curious tradition decisions were invariably unanimous. One duty of the assembly was to allot strips of land to individual households at the periodical redistributions. Another was to elect a village elder (*starosta*) for a period of three years. The holder of this unpopular office presided over meetings, and was responsible for collecting the tax imposed on the commune as a whole. He might, like the officious Antip Sedelnikov in Chekhov's *Peasants*, confiscate the samovar of an offending household as a means of enforcing the payment of arrears, or even lock up an old woman for swearing at a village meeting. On a less grotesque level, he was also responsible for the call-up of peasants into the forces, had the duty of reporting suspicious strangers to the police, and could arrest criminals. As a badge of office he wore a bronze medallion on a chain round his neck.

A peasant was not permitted to leave his own area without a passport, and this could not be issued without the permission of the head of household (unless the applicant were himself the head of a household) and also of the village assembly. Moreover, even the passport-holding absentee peasant remained compulsorily attached to his commune, still responsible for paying his share of the collectively imposed tax.

CANTONS Under the emancipation provisions communes were grouped together in large, newly established units termed cantons (*volosti*). A typical canton was a collection of small villages. It too had its elder (*volostnoy starshina*), as well as a clerk. Perhaps the only person in the cantonal administration able to read and write, the clerk sometimes wielded more power than was intended. The cantonal assembly, which elected the cantonal elder and other officials, consisted of the elders of the component communes, and one representative from each ten households. Apart from its administrative responsibilities, the canton formed a court to try minor cases involving peasants – the only judicial organ which retained the right to award corporal punishment after 1863. Members of the gentry holding property within the boundaries of a given canton and commune were, it need hardly be said, not themselves subject to cantonal or communal authority; nor were professional persons such as doctors and schoolteachers.

Since continued liability to corporal punishment, together with the other above-mentioned restrictions, affected only the peasantry, these remained subject to special discriminations even after emancipation. They were still at a disadvantage, even if notably less so than under serfdom. Hence the claim made by some historians that, after emancipation, the peasant exchanged bondage to a landowner for bondage to the commune.

In 1889, as part of Alexander III's 'counter-reforms', the canton's powers were limited – to the peasants' further disadvantage – by the appointment of newly instituted officials with the title of land captain (*zemsky nachalnik*). It was laid down that these should be drawn wherever possible from the local hereditary landed gentry, and they received wide discretionary powers. They could arrest or suspend peasant officials and impose fines without trial. But Florinsky exaggerates when he claims that 'a sham of self-government was preserved, yet peasant Russia was actually ruled by petty officials drawn from the midst of the landed nobility and controlled by the minister of the interior' (Florinsky, ii, p. 1095). On the other hand, Mackenzie Wallace, admittedly writing before the institution of land captains, had gone too far in the opposite direction by calling village communes 'capital specimens of representative Constitutional government of the extreme democratic type' (Mackenzie Wallace, i, pp. 192–3). The truth lay somewhere between these statements.

10 Landowners and gentlemen

STATUS AND ORGANISATION   The gentry's importance in Russian culture is completely out of proportion to its numbers – just over one per cent of the population at the end of the nineteenth century. Much Russian literature was written by landowners for landowners about landowners, and by the time of Turgenev the squire's country seat, such as the 'nest of gentlefolk' in the title of one of his novels, had become an established setting for Russian fiction.

Two overlapping concepts are involved, those of landowner (*pomeshchik*) and gentleman (*dvoryanin*), the latter term denoting membership of one of the estates into which society was divided. It is sometimes rendered 'noble', so that Turgenev's novel may be alluded to as *A Nest of Noblemen*, but since the English word nobility implies possession of a title, the less misleading term gentry is preferred here.

Before 1861 a provision (often circumvented, like all Russian provisions) existed whereby no one except a gentleman could own serfs, and as land tenure was usually combined with serf-ownership, a large landowner at the time of serfdom was almost inevitably a member of the gentry class. After emancipation there was a progressive decrease in the amount of land held by the gentry, whose holdings passed more and more to members of other classes. Thus Chekhov's *Cherry Orchard*, in which Lopakhin, the self-made son of a former serf, buys a vast estate from feckless genteel owners, seems to sum up over a hundred years of decline from the late eighteenth century under Catherine the Great, the gentry's golden age.

The estate of the gentry could be entered by non-gentlemen who attained high rank in the civil service or armed forces. Though the specific grade conferring this right varied according to the regulations currently in force, the important point is that the estate was not exclusive, as some of its members would have liked to make it. Certain civil and military awards – those of St Vladimir and St George, as also the first class of other decorations – likewise conveyed the status of hereditary membership of the gentry. An inferior grade of gentry was that conferred by the status of individual, as opposed to hereditary, gentleman. This status was conferred by lower rank than that which gave hereditary gentry status, and, as the title implies, did not devolve to children.

The Emperors relied on the gentry to resist revolution and support the *status quo*. One of Nicholas I's police chiefs, Dubelt, summed up the position as follows: 'The landowner is the most reliable bulwark of the sovereign. . . . If his power is destroyed, the people will become a flood, endangering in time even the Tsar himself. . . . The landlord is the most faithful, the unsleeping watchdog of the state; he is the natural police-magistrate (quoted in Sumner, p. 142). The landowners' privileges were intended to preserve their loyalty and encourage them in the performance of specific services. Themselves exempt from flogging, conscription and personal taxation during the period when these inconveniences remained in force, they were responsible under serfdom for collecting the poll-tax paid by their peasants, for drafting them into the army and for administering local justice – functions which all passed to the village commune or to the canton after 1861.

The gentry had an elaborate corporate organisation, including assemblies at provincial and district level, presided over by marshals of the gentry who were chosen through a combination of election by their peers with appointment by the ministry of the interior. One of their duties was to keep delinquent gentlemen in order. In Chekhov's story *My Life* (1896) the provincial marshal of the gentry reports the hero, Misail Poloznev, to the governor of the province for working as a labourer – conduct unbecoming in a gentleman and son of the local architect.

After the local government reforms of 1864, the marshals of the gentry became *ex officio* chairmen of the assemblies of the newly instituted rural councils, the zemstvos. The institution of land captains appointed from among the gentry in 1889 (see above, p. 921) was another provision whereby the landowning gentry regained some of the control over peasant affairs lost at the time of emancipation.

TITLES   The Russians had a titled nobility or aristocracy, but it formed only a small section of the gentry as a whole. Their oldest hereditary title was that of prince (*knyaz*), and many Russian princes traced their descent from Ryurik, said to have died in AD 879. He was traditionally the founder of the first Russian ruling house, that of the Ryurikids, which reigned until 1598. Other princes were descended from Gedimin of Lithuania, or from Tatar or Georgian potentates. Members of the Tsar's family held the title *veliky knyaz* (literally 'great prince'), for which grand duke is used in English. Prince was the only Russian title in use in the nineteenth century that dated from before Peter the Great, who introduced new grades of nobility: those of count (*graf*) and baron. The latter title was held by many members of the German nobility in the Russian Baltic, who so often reached high rank in the administration. It was also awarded to successful Russian businessmen, for which reason princes and counts tended to look down on it.

By contrast with English practice, titles were inherited by all the children of a titled father, whence the large number of princes, princesses, counts and countesses in Russian novels. It was also usual for property to be split among all the sons of a family, not left exclusively to the eldest – hence a tendency for members of the aristocracy to be poorer than their rank suggests. There was nothing implausible in Dostoyevsky's beginning his *Idiot* by introducing a penniless Prince Myshkin almost in the role of beggar and suppliant, while if the name of a Prince Golitsyn cropped up in real life, the question was apt to be asked: 'Who is this Golitsyn? A rich one or a poor one?' (Blum, p. 376).

DRESS Peter the Great had compelled the gentry to dress like western Europeans by wearing what the peasants called 'German clothes', whereas clergy, merchants and peasants continued to wear traditional Russian dress. In the nineteenth century this differentiation was maintained. The heroine of Pushkin's *Young Lady as Peasant*, one of his *Tales of Belkin*, was accordingly able to pass herself off as a peasant girl only after getting her maids to stitch her a rustic shirt and *sarafan* for the occasion. While remaining distinct from the clothing of other classes, the dress of the gentry did of course change according to changes in fashion. For ladies it was full skirts in the thirties and crinolines in the sixties. At the beginning of the nineteenth century men were wearing tail-coats. These continued as formal wear, but were ousted for more ordinary occasions by frock-coats and later by jackets and dinner-jackets, as

were top-hats by bowlers. Waistcoats were considered essential wear
for a gentleman. By the end of the nineteenth century, dress distinctions were becoming less marked – that is, gentry and non-
gentry townspeople were dressing more and more alike.

USE OF FRENCH   As readers of Tolstoy's *War and Peace* will remember, French was a common means of communication between
gentlefolk at the beginning of the nineteenth century – many educated Russians spoke it far better than their own language. Pushkin,
in a sense, knew Russian better than anyone else before or since,
yet he regularly wrote to his wife, also a Russian, in French. Herzen
explains that his father wrote better French than Russian and would
never so much as read a Russian book. He did once embark on
Karamzin's *History of the Russian State*, hearing that Alexander I
had read it, but soon laid it down, saying: 'All these Izyaslaviches
and Olgoviches – what a bore!' (*My Past and Thoughts*, ch. v). After
the discovery of Anna Karenin's adultery, her husband found it convenient to speak to her in French – *vous* seemed chilly enough to
express his disapproval, whereas use of the Russian *vy* (the distant
or polite second person plural) would have involved too harsh a
transition from the intimate *ty*. Dostoyevsky, an extreme Russian
nationalist, objected to the practice of bringing up genteel infants
to speak French: 'Little does Mama realise that she is administering
deadly poison to her two-year-old child when she employs a French
bonne to look after him' (*Diary of a Writer*, May–June 1877).

In time the use of French declined socially, and it was almost
a genteel vulgarism by Chekhov's day. It is typical that some of
his non-approved characters, including Natasha in *Three Sisters*
(1900–1), should speak inaccurate French. The habit of using
French first names instead of Russian, for instance of addressing an
Ivan as *Jean*, had also become a sign of social pretentiousness.

IMPROVIDENCE AND ECCENTRICITY   The gentry varied from
impoverished squires, barely distinguishable in their way of life
from their own few miserable serfs, to the largest serf-owners in
the country. In the early nineteenth century a Count D.N. Shere-
metev owned nearly three hundred thousand serfs. His debts were
on the same heroic scale – he is said to have owed six million roubles
in 1859 (Blum, pp. 370, 379).

Huge debts were almost a status symbol to the landowner, and
any mention of a country estate in nineteenth-century literature is

likely to be followed by the information that it is heavily mortgaged and that its owner faces imminent bankruptcy. When emancipation took place, on the basis of redemption payments for land to be made by the peasants at rates favouring the landowners, this money was advanced to the owners by the government. Much of it was then swallowed up to meet their debts, and much was squandered on ostentatious sprees in the watering-places of Europe. These antics greatly irritated Dostoyevsky, a frequent visitor to western Europe. According to him the Russian landowner, with his vast retinue of maids and governesses, aroused the envy of observers from other countries, who did not realise that he was wasting the last of his fortune on such ostentation.

These sybarites who lounge about German spas and the shores of Swiss lakes, these Luculli consuming their substance in Parisian restaurants – they themselves know, and even with some degree of pain foresee, that they will run through their entire funds in the end, and that their children, these same little cherubs in English costumes, will perhaps have to beg alms throughout Europe, or become French or German labourers. (Dostoyevsky, *Diary of a Writer*, May–June 1877).

Landowners' improvidence was encouraged by the government, which set up special banks to help the gentry and rescue it from the clutches of private money-lenders. There were even arrangements whereby charitable foundations loaned large sums to landowners out of funds subscribed for philanthropic purposes. Money lent to some landowners was in effect a concealed gift. For a plebeian to enforce payment from a gentleman was, to put it mildly, difficult, since many an upper-class Russian agreed with Count Vronsky in *Anna Karenin* that gambling debts were the only financial obligations to be taken seriously by a man of honour.

To improvidence must be added laziness and personal eccentricity. Foreign observers were amazed at the hordes of servants with which Russian gentlefolk surrounded themselves, and this in an age when the upper class everywhere had a profusion of servants by later standards. Waited on hand and foot, not stooping even to fill their own tobacco-pipes, Russian landowners sometimes resembled vegetables more than sentient beings. Such are the two old people portrayed in Gogol's *Old World Landowners* in his collection of stories *Mirgorod*. Such too is the sleepy atmosphere of the

Russian countryside in *Oblomov's Dream*, the celebrated chapter from Goncharov's novel depicting his lethargic hero's childhood on an estate where he is spoiled by relatives and servants in an over-protected atmosphere. The publication of *Oblomov* almost coincided with the end of serfdom, but the post-emancipation estate in Goncharov's later novel *The Precipice* has an atmosphere comparably slumberous.

Eccentric as the grotesque landowners in Gogol's *Dead Souls* are, there is ample competition from other works such as Saltykov-Shchedrin's *Old Days in Poshekhonye* and *The Golovlyov Family*, portraying freakish squires before and after emancipation. A real-life specimen from the early nineteenth century was F.I. Tolstoy, nicknamed 'the American' – Herzen explains that he once made his wife, a gipsy singer, stand on a table while he put a shot through the heel of her shoe to display his marksmanship. He once seized a humble citizen with whom he was annoyed, bound him hand and foot and wrenched out one of his teeth. When the victim later dared to make an official complaint, Tolstoy bribed the police and the man was imprisoned for lodging false information. As Herzen so aptly comments: 'The stifling emptiness and dumbness of Russian life, curiously combined with its vitality and rumbustious character, give rise to all sorts of crackpot outbursts in our midst' (*My Past and Thoughts*, ch. xiv). When Dostoyevsky's villain Stavrogin (in *Devils*) pulls a respectable middle-aged gentleman across the floor of the local club by his nose and is later found biting the ear of the pro-vincial governor, his behaviour is, therefore, almost traditional in an ex-officer and gentleman. So too is that of Nozdryov in Gogol's *Dead Souls* when he orders his servants to flog Chichikov for refusing to finish a game of draughts in which he was being cheated. Such genteel pranks continued to enliven Russian life and fiction throughout the period studied here, for 'a Russian', as Dostoyevsky's narrator had commented in *Devils*, 'takes incredible delight in every kind of scandalous public upheaval'.

TREATMENT OF SERFS Nineteenth-century landowners' powers over their serfs remained almost as uncontrolled as Catherine the Great had once told Diderot: 'Landowners do whatever seems good to them on their estates except inflict capital punishment; that is forbidden' (quoted in Sumner, p. 145). Even that provision was evaded since serfs were sometimes flogged to death.

A brief but telling episode relating to flogging and landowner–serf relation is recounted in Turgenev's *Manager*, one of his *Sportsman's Sketches*. A young squire and retired guards officer, Arkady Pavlovich Penochkin, is served with claret which turns out not to have been properly *chambré* by one of the servants, Fyodor. With no emotion and barely pausing from the polite conversation in which he is engaged, the master rings for another flunkey, a fat, low-browed creature, and gives the instruction: 'About Fyodor … do the necessary' (i.e. flog him). He then turns back to his guest, blandly remarking: '*Voilà, mon cher, les désagréments de la campagne*'. The most eloquent feature of this episode is that the punishment is ordered so casually and without, as it were, even the excuse of sadism.

The catalogue of landowners' outrages against serfs could be much extended. Siberian exile might be imposed by whim, as by Turgenev's mother on two of her villagers for failing to bow to her. Turgenev himself, a humane man whose *Sportsman's Sketches* may well have advanced the cause of emancipation, is reported to have paid seven hundred roubles for a serf concubine to console him during exile to his country estate. More enterprising landowners kept entire harems of serf women. A market for serf girls, brought from various parts of Russia, existed in the industrial centre of Ivanovo for the benefit of textile tycoons, including industrialists who were themselves serfs (Blum, p. 427).

At the time of serfdom, landowners could prevent the marriage of serfs or make it conditional on paying a fee. They could force a man and woman to marry against their will, though such a project might be thwarted if the couple heard of it in good time and could arrange to become godparents of the same child – which meant that they were debarred from marrying each other by ecclesiastical law. Some landowners threatened serfs with unwelcome marriages or conscription in order to extort money from them, having discreetly enquired into their means beforehand so as to know how much to charge. Though owners could connive at the acquisition of serfs by their own serfs, there was nothing to prevent them from re-possessing such property when they wished. Another deplorable device was to 'free' serfs grown too old for work, which simply meant turning them out to fend for themselves. Serfs were, accordingly, sometimes treated worse than domestic animals.

Under Alexander I and Nicholas I attempts were made to limit landowners' powers by provisions against arbitrary injustice. It became illegal to break up serf families by sale, to sell serfs at public auction, to sell them without land – all of which regulations were of course widely evaded. Having no effective process of appeal against landowners, serfs could not even enforce such meagre legal rights as they possessed. Hence the many outbreaks of peasant violence – about eight hundred in the years 1845 to 1860 – and the numerous murders of landowners and their managers by serfs.

Many were the absentee landlords who, in extreme cases, might never have visited their estates, or who confined themselves, like Oblomov, to communicating with their bailiffs. But others were eager to improve their properties and introduce modern methods. Journals and societies were formed to promote agriculture. This left most squires untouched, but the 'good' landowner does figure in fiction, trying to bridge the communication gap between squire and peasant. Tolstoy's experiences with his own peasants provided material for much of his writing from the early *Morning of a Landowner* (1856) onwards, and two examples of his 'good' landowners are mentioned above (p. 90). That a late-nineteenth-century landowner need not necessarily be lazy and feckless is shown by Alyokhin, the hard-working squire in Chekhov's story *About Love* (1898).

Beside monsters of idleness, profligacy, cruelty and eccentricity, the Russian gentry also produced many humane and sensitive men, including the very writers who portray the faults of their own kind with such skill. As the most articulate class, the gentry dominated cultural and intellectual life, even providing its own destroyers. That a leading anarchist, Peter Kropotkin, should have been a prince and cousin to a governor-general assassinated by a terrorist; that Sophia Perovsky, one of Alexander II's assassins, should have been a provincial governor's daughter; that Lenin himself should have been a hereditary gentleman – none of this will surprise those attuned to the rhythms of the period. Wide indeed was the range of activity or inactivity attained by scions of the Russian squirearchy, from the near-paralysis of the fictional Oblomov to the active real-life Bakunin, escapee from Siberia, stoker of the fires of European revolution and rival of Karl Marx within the First Socialist International.

11 *Religion*

CHURCH AND STATE   The Empire had an established religion, Russian Orthodoxy, of which the Tsar was the official defender, and in a sense the head. But his position was not comparable to that of the Pope in the Roman Catholic Church. The Tsar's function was to protect dogma, but he was not empowered to change it, and though he attended divine service, he could not officiate.

Just as the state became increasingly multinational through territorial expansion, so expansion also rendered it increasingly multi-religious. The accession of the Baltic lands had brought in many additional Protestants, and the annexations of Poland introduced Catholic and Jewish citizens, of whom there had previously been very few. Then the conquest of Central Asia enlarged the Muslim component. But the Orthodox Church remained predominant, as is shown by the following breakdown of the population in percentages relating to the beginning of the twentieth century (from Kovalevsky, p. 66):

Orthodox	71 per cent
Catholic	9 per cent
Protestant	5 per cent
Jewish	3 per cent
Muslim	9 per cent

The figure for Orthodox Christians may be misleading, since it unavowedly includes many persons (the so-called Old Believers) explicitly opposed to the official Orthodox faith and also sectarians, who had no links with Orthodoxy at all. The numbers of Old Believers and sectarians are hard to establish owing to a strong tendency to minimise their importance in official estimates. Some authorities have even put the figure as high as twenty or twenty-five million, though the total was recorded as barely two million in the 1897 census (Kolarz, pp. 128–9). Still, whatever the true figure may be, the Orthodox Church was certainly numerically dominant, as well as representing the official state religion.

It had held this position since AD 988, when Vladimir, Grand Prince of Kiev, made Christianity the official religion of Old Russia. When the Greek and Roman churches divided in 1054, the Russians sided with the former, a decision of great consequence to their cultural history, which thereafter developed along different lines from that of western Europe. But the Russian Church did not remain a subordinate branch of the Greek, and when Constantinople was captured by the Turks in 1453 Russia became ecclesiastically independent in practice. This independence was formalised in 1589, when the office of Patriarch of Moscow was created. In 1721 the patriarchate was abolished by Peter the Great, who replaced it with a new institution, the Most Holy Governing Synod – until 1917 the governing body of the Russian Orthodox Church. The secularisation of church lands was completed in 1764.

Of the church's submissiveness to the state in the nineteenth century many instances can be quoted. While insurgent troops were defying the Tsar in St Petersburg during the Decembrist revolt, 'many of the clergy of the capital, with the metropolitan at their head, went in full vestments, cross in hand, to urge the rebels to submit' (Curtiss, p. 30). The Metropolitan Filaret of Moscow, a notoriously reactionary prelate, opposed the abolition of flogging – and of serfdom too, but changed his mind at the last moment and helped to draw up the emancipation manifesto of 1861. After Turgenev's death in 1883, young priests were required by the Synod and bishops to curb their enthusiasm, as expressed in obituary sermons, for this representative of Russian liberalism – an episode which at least shows that not all elements in the Orthodox Church were entirely subservient to the state.

THE ORTHODOX CHURCH IN LITERATURE   Of the better-known nineteenth-century authors, Leskov covers the richness and variety of Russian religion especially fully in many stories and sketches, his descriptions being by no means confined to the official church, but also including numerous sketches of Old Believers. He gives a particularly detailed picture of a priest's tribulations in the novel *Cathedral Folk*. Another sympathetic portrait of a church dignitary is *The Bishop* (1902) by Chekhov – who, though himself an atheist, was far from anti-clerical, but accepted the Orthodox Church as an integral feature of Russian life and culture. Tolstoy was less co-operatively disposed. He left a scathing satire on Orthodox Church ritual in *Resurrection*, and his non-fictional religious works, such as *Confession* (first published in Geneva in 1884), *A Criticism of Dogmatic Theology* and *What I Believe*, could not be brought out in Russia at the time they were written. It will also be remembered that Tolstoy enjoyed the distinction of being excommunicated in 1901. His clash with the church derives from his advocacy of rational Christianity based on Gospel teaching, but free from later accretions. The Orthodox Church with its spectacular ritual was far removed from his concept of religion.

ORGANISATION As the governing body of the church, the Synod consisted of ecclesiastical dignitaries, but did not have a fixed number of members. The Metropolitan of St Petersburg was usually its chairman and the Metropolitans of Moscow and Kiev were also members, as was the Exarch of Georgia. Other members included archbishops, bishops or abbots appointed by the Tsar, and two senior members of the white clergy (see p. 104), one of whom was usually the Tsar's confessor. But the key figure, also appointed by the Tsar, was a layman – the so-called chief procurator, whose approval was required for all the Synod's decisions and who became in all but name a governmental minister for religion – indeed, he was accorded the official status of minister. A particularly notable, not to say notorious, chief procurator was Konstantin Pobedonostsev – as already mentioned, one of the most powerful figures in Russia after the Tsar during his tenure of office (1880–1905). The Synod controlled higher church appointments, ecclesiastical schools and ecclesiastical censorship. It ensured that the church remained a docile instrument of the state throughout the nineteenth century.

There were about sixty dioceses in all, of which three – those of St Petersburg, Moscow and Kiev – came under metropolitans, while nineteen were archbishoprics and the rest bishoprics. Within each diocese a consistory and chancery, with a lay secretary responsible to the chief procurator, ensured that policy percolated to individual parishes. The consistory administered church schools and seminaries within the diocese and was responsible for the ecclesiastical courts in which divorce cases were heard.

THE ORTHODOX CLERGY   Though the clergy was long classed with
the gentry as 'privileged' by exemption from personal taxation, recruitment into the army and corporal punishment (see p. 76), clerical enjoyment of these concessions tended, for various reasons, to
be limited. Certainly no one familiar with western European conditions was likely to consider the Russian parish priest a privileged
person.

The clergy fell into two classes, popularly termed white and black.
The black clergy consisted of monks dedicated to celibacy, while
for white clergy marriage was not only permitted, but was a compulsory condition for ordination. A priest must marry a spinster and
was not permitted a second marriage – if his wife died he must either
leave the church or become one of its minor officers, such as a deacon,
verger or sacristan – these functionaries too were members of the
clerical estate. Though the black clergy indeed did wear black
clothes, it would be wrong to infer that members of the white clergy
were therefore clad in white, for they too wore black or at least sub-
fusc. Both had full beards and kept their hair long. Only members
of the black clergy might aspire to high office as abbot, archiman-
drite, bishop, archbishop or metropolitan, whereas a white cleric
must remain a humble parish priest denied promotion beyond the
rank of senior priest, or of superintendent priest with supervisory
duties over several parishes.

As the following figures show, the nineteenth century saw a decline in the numbers of the clergy in relation to the population
as a whole. The numbers of the white clergy also declined absolutely,
while an increase in the actual numbers of the black did not keep
pace with the growth of the population (from Milyukov, i, p. 147).

	Actual figures		As per 100,000 inhabitants of Orthodox faith	
	1840	1890	1840	1890
White clergy	116,728	96,892	265	137
Monks, nuns and novices	15,251	40,286	56	34

The clergy almost formed a caste within Russian society. Any
'white' priest was likely to be a priest's son and to be married to
a priest's daughter, their children being educated separately from
the population at large in special teaching establishments. Though
not closed to children from other estates, these were free to the

clergy – church schools (*dukhovnyye uchilishcha*) for younger boys, and then seminaries for older, the latter being a combined upper school and college. There were also special diocesan schools for daughters of the clergy. Would-be white seminarists sought to marry priests' daughters who, with luck, might bring the parish of a defunct or retired father as a dowry, assuming that the bishop and his consistory (who tended to acquire the function of unofficial marriage brokers) approved. The black clergy too was recruited from the seminaries, where young men faced a stark choice: either an ambitious church career or married bliss, but not both.

Provisions made under Alexander II to throw the church open to entrants from outside the clergy did not lead to a rush of applicants, and seminarists continued to provide most new recruits. But though nearly all priests were ex-seminarists, it by no means follows that all seminarists became priests. Many joined the anti-clerical intelligentsia, and some figured in literature – it will be remembered that two of Russia's best-known radical thinkers and literary critics, Dobrolyubov and Chernyshevsky, were sons of priests. The most famous seminarist of all time, and one acclaimed by some as a universal genius, was the product of a nineteenth-century Georgian theological college who happened not to be a priest's son – Joseph Stalin, then known as Dzhugashvili. As his career suggests, church schools and seminaries were not always successful in instilling conventional piety, but were sometimes more effective in promoting violence and cruelty. This is emphasised in one especially well-known mid-century account: *Sketches of a Church School* (1862–3) by N.G. Pomyalovsky. An ex-seminarist, the author drank himself to death when he was twenty-eight, and his book reflects memories of school-days more unseemly than Tom Brown's.

Seminarists were prominent in the student protest movement from the 1860s onwards. In 1885 the Metropolitan of Moscow called in the police to quell rioting seminarists, who were severely beaten in his presence with rods which, according to rumour, he had personally consecrated for the purpose. A few years later the seminarists of Voronezh attempted to blow up their rector with a bomb placed in a stove (Leroy-Beaulieu, pp. 269–70). The Russian seminary thus moved with the times, and it is not surprising that it was sometimes thought of as a nursery of revolution.

Once established in a parish, the priest might well find his new surroundings no more edifying than his college. He might occupy the humble hut which had belonged to his predecessor, now perhaps his father-in-law. He might also be allotted a few acres of land which he could cultivate, like his parishioners, or rent out if he wished. But he had no staple income. Though the state dispensed meagre funds for the upkeep of parish priests, many received nothing, for such subsidies were generally channelled to parishes where competition from some rival persuasion had to be taken into account. Hence the practice whereby the priest made charges for christening, marrying, burying and so on. Since there was no fixed tariff, it was usual to haggle over the price. There were, accordingly, stories of young people presenting themselves at church to be married, but departing unwed after failing to strike a bargain with the priest. Underpaid for a blessing, some priests were quite capable of substituting a curse.

On major holidays, especially Christmas and Easter, the priest would tour his parish resplendent in chasuble and stole, and accompanied by various minions. Entering each hut in turn, he would face the icon, intone a prayer or two, pocket what was in effect a tip, and move on. It was of such ministrations that Chekhov wrote in *Peasants*: 'Those who had not fasted and prepared for communion in Lent were charged fifteen copecks apiece by the parish priest when he went round the huts with the cross at Easter.'

Sometimes the priest's steps became noticeably unsteady as these processions continued. Russian peasants had crude notions of hospitality, and to refuse a glass or two of their vodka was to give grave offence. This was not in any case an insult which many priests were temperamentally inclined to offer, and the result might be that they staggered round their parishes hopelessly drunk. On the following day the very peasant who had been most insistent in plying his priest with liquor would be the first to mock his inability to hold it. Herzen has a story of a parish priest so dedicated to his pastoral duties that, after officiating at a wedding or christening in an outlying village, he was often carried off unconscious by the peasants, and dumped in his cart like a sheaf of corn to be taken home by his horse, which knew the way back without needing a driver (*My Past and Thoughts*, ch. xxviii).

Not all priests were drunkards, as the prevalence of such anecdotes might suggest. They are less misleading, perhaps, as an index of the genial disrespect in which many a priest was held by his flock, though his status in the towns might be less lowly than in the country. The Russian landowner looked down on the priest as an inferior, and was perfectly capable of having him ducked in the village pond to provide amusement for his guests. Peasants thought it unlucky to meet a priest in the street and coined sayings to illustrate the greed of the *pop* (the disrespectful word by which the parish priest, more politely termed *svyashchennik*, was known). But there were other even lowlier figures among the clergy. The deacon or priest's assistant, who helped to perform services, could himself carry out certain functions such as conducting funerals, and was expected to have a rich bass voice. Yet humbler were the minor clerical officers, consisting of sextons, bell-ringers, psalm-singers and readers. Persons of all these categories had the right to send their children to the free church schools and seminaries.

Though village priests and their minions were often regarded with tolerant contempt, it is important to note that Russian peasants by no means transferred to religion itself the feelings with which they often regarded its representatives.

APPEARANCE AND DECORATION OF CHURCHES Orthodox churches were rectangular in plan, or cruciform, and might have a number of onion-domes, gilded or painted in a bright colour, usually blue or green, and surmounted by a Greek cross. There might be a bell-tower. The chancel or sanctuary, that is the eastern part of the church for the use of the officiating priest and his assistants, is confusingly termed *altar* in Russian. The altar itself is called a throne (*prestol*). The chancel is separated from the body of the church by a screen on which icons are hung, called the iconostasis and containing three doors, of which the central one is the 'Tsar's gate', through which only the priest may pass. In front of this on the congregation's side is a raised platform, the ambo, from which prayers, readings and sermons are delivered. If there was a special choir to supplement the singing of the priests and servitors, it would normally be housed in a balcony at the back (west end) of the church.

Much importance was attached to the cult of icons, consisting of half-length paintings of Jesus Christ, the Madonna or saints, executed in a stylised manner originally deriving from Byzantine tradition. They varied in size from about a square inch to several square feet, and the part of the picture representing clothes might be covered with ornamental metal. Humble icons were manufactured in tens of thousands by the cottage industry of Vladimir province, and, as mentioned above, no peasant hut was complete without its icon. More valuable icons, often richly embellished, were found in churches, including miracle-working icons, the object of their own special cult. Some, including the Kazan Madonna, had feast days in their honour. Others, such as the Smolensk Madonna, which accompanied the Russian army during the war against Napoleon in 1812, were associated with martial glory and credited with such triumphs as the French retreat from Moscow. The Vladimir Madonna had reputedly saved Moscow from the Tatars. Icons were sometimes paraded round the fields to discourage drought. During the anti-Jewish pogroms at the end of the nineteenth century it was prudent to keep an icon available, since to display it was to signal to the rampaging mob that one was a co-religionist, and thus an inappropriate candidate for insult, injury, looting, rape or death at the hands of one's brothers in Christ.

Icons were displayed in churches and – as in private homes – commonly had a lamp burning in front of them. Candles too were prominent in the church, both decoratively and financially. It was usual for the congregation to buy candles, often manufactured by the church as a source of revenue. The glitter of lamps and candles, the stylised beauty of the icons, the magnificent vestments of priests and acolytes, the superb singing and the solemn atmosphere of the service – all combined to lend majesty to Orthodox Church services. In a small village the ritual was naturally less imposing than in a major monastery or metropolitan cathedral, but the service gave the ill-used Russian peasant a glimpse of something magically different from his daily life.

SERVICES, RITUAL AND SACRAMENTS   Officiating clergy and their assistants wore a surplice, the *stikhar*. Over this the priest wore a chasuble or sleeveless robe, while deacons wore a stole on one shoulder. A different kind of stole was worn by the priest under his chasuble, over both shoulders. As headgear the priest wore a soft hat of black or purple velvet, pointed on top (the *skufya*), or a tall hat (the *kamilavka*). A bishop wore a mitre and a long cope, and carried a crozier.

At Orthodox services the congregation stood, and there were no pews, organs or statues. Singing by clergy and choir, unaccompanied by instruments or congregation, occupied a prominent part in the service. A linguistically sophisticated visitor would detect that, though any sermon would be delivered in Russian, the liturgy was couched in a different but related tongue, Church Slavonic. The visitor would also notice that the liturgy was phenomenally time-consuming.

Confession was soon over, but was by no means considered a formality, even though special confessional boxes were not provided. Parishioners often queued up to confess, and each would answer one or two questions, after which he would receive absolution with the laying of a corner of the priest's stole on his head. Then he would kiss the Cross and Gospel, and give his name to the deacon, who kept a list. At communion the members of the congregation partook of both bread and wine. The bread, in the form of specially baked small loaves (*prosfory*), was broken in pieces and placed in the wine, 'intinction' being the technical name for this procedure. The priest would ladle a spoonful of wine, containing a piece of the soaked bread, into the mouth of each communicant, who would take another piece of the bread and consume it as he turned away. A peasant described in Dostoyevsky's *Diary of a Writer* (1873, ch. v) was induced, for a 'dare', to smuggle his pellet of wine-soaked bread out of church and aim a shot-gun at it after it had been placed on a post – perhaps the most grotesque among the same author's many descriptions of sacrilegious acts.

The Orthodox wedding ceremony was elaborate. Bride and bridegroom wore crowns, exchanged rings, drank three times alternately from the same cup and were paraded three times round the church, their hands clasped for them by the priest. A well-known fictional description of an Orthodox wedding – that of Levin and Kitty Oblonsky – occurs in Tolstoy's *Anna Karenin*. Christening was combined with confirmation, and triple total immersion was the practice. At funeral services the dead were exposed to view in open coffins – a procedure which made it possible for Hermann, hero of Pushkin's *Queen of Spades* (1834), to receive the impression that his victim, a deceased countess, winked at him when he bowed his farewell to her on the occasion of her funeral.

The most important church festival was Easter, with which many traditional practices, culinary, liturgical and osculatory, were associated. The Easter kiss exchanged between members of the congregation at the end of the service on Easter eve and the prescribed dialogue ('Christ has arisen'; 'In truth he has arisen') form an episode in the seduction of Catherine Maslov in Tolstoy's *Resurrection*.

MONKS   Though only monks could rise to high ecclesiastical office, the average monk was a humble individual lacking such ambition or opportunity. Despite the importance of monasteries in earlier Russian history, monks and nuns, numbering in 1890 only about forty thousand of both sexes (with a preponderance of nuns) were remarkably few in number and simple in organisation. They had only one monastic rule and many monasteries and convents were small. But three were large and outstanding, being called *lavry* and associated with a past or present capital of Russia. These were the Monastery of the Caves at Kiev, the Monastery of the Trinity and St Sergius near Moscow, and the Monastery of St Alexander Nevsky at St Petersburg. Other famous monasteries included a fourth *lavra*, that of Pochayev in the western Ukraine, the Solovetsky Monastery on islands in the White Sea, and that of Optina Pustyn in central Russia. The last-named was noted for an institution which interested Dostoyevsky: that of tutorship by older monks termed elders (*startsy*). The best-known monastery in Russian fiction is that in *The Brothers Karamazov*. Here Dostoyevsky portrays a young novice, Alyosha Karamazov, and the influence exercised over him by the *starets* Father Zosima, who had been an army officer before entering the monastery. Another well-known fictional recruit to the life of religious hermit was also a former army officer – Tolstoy's Father Sergius in his posthumous story of the same name.

OLD BELIEVERS   The Old Believers, sometimes called Old Ritualists or Schismatics, were an important social and religious phenomenon. They originated with the schism which occurred in the Russian Orthodox Church in 1667, when approval was given to the revision of Russian church books undertaken at the instigation of the Patriarch Nikon by collation with the Greek originals from which they were derived, but from which they had since greatly diverged. Old Believers were those who rejected the newly corrected versions, clinging to various archaic practices which came to distinguish them from the Orthodox. Old Belief rallied Russian conservatism and distrust of foreigners, whether Greek or not, among the less educated, but the issues dividing Orthodoxy and Old Belief now seem utterly trivial. Thus the Old Believers crossed themselves with two fingers and sang Hallelujah twice, while the Orthodox crossed themselves with three fingers and sang Hallelujah thrice. There were differences in pronouncing the name Jesus, in the depiction of the Cross, and so on. In the early days of the Schism remarkably large numbers of Old Believers expressed their religious fervour by shutting themselves in their wooden churches or huts and burning themselves alive. Many were the martyrs who went to the stake or had their tongues ripped out rather than cross themselves in non-approved style. Such punishment was not imposed in the nineteenth century, but severe discrimination and persecution continued. Old Believers were also conservative outside the context of ritual. They had defied Peter the Great by keeping their beards and old-fashioned caftans. They were mainly of Great Russian origin and consisted of peasants, merchants and Cossacks – rarely of gentry. They eschewed tobacco and also – though not total abstainers – drinking orgies. Many succeeded in business, building palatial residences in Moscow, and their sobriety and business acumen have caused them to be compared with English Quakers and Methodists. They have been claimed as quintessentially Russian and their main centres were in the suburbs of Moscow, regarded as a more Russian city than St Petersburg. Outside the Moscow area there were numerous Old Believers in the north of European Russia, on the Volga, and also among the miners of the Urals, the Cossacks of the south-east of European Russia and the colonisers of Siberia.

The Old Believers were a mixed group, falling into two main classes according to whether they made use of priests or not. It happened that there were no Old Believer bishops for two centuries after the outbreak of the Schism, which made it impossible to ordain Old Believer priests. A section of Old Believers known as 'priestists' (*popovtsy*) therefore relied on 'runaway' Orthodox priests to perform marriage services and other sacraments. In the 1860s they secured the services of a co-operative Orthodox prelate, Metropolitan Ambrose of the Church of Bosnia, who consecrated three Old Believers as bishops at Bela Krinica, then on Austrian territory. The ordination of Old Believer priests thus became possible and ensured for the future, but not all 'priestists' would accept Bela Krinica and a minority of 'runaway-priestists' continued as before. The 'priestless' were a less organised group. They had no sacraments or marriage, tended to believe that the reign of Antichrist had come about on earth, expected the imminent end of the world, and avoided persons of other religious persuasions.

Old Believers figure in Leskov's *Sealed Angel* (1873), which recounts the adventures of an icon confiscated by the police and restored to the faithful by a miracle. The greatest fictional chronicler of Old Belief is P.I. Melnikov-Pechersky, whose long novels *In the Forests* (1871–5) and *In the Hills* (1875–81) describe their communities on the Volga.

OTHER DENOMINATIONS AND SECTARIANS   The religious 'sects', of which a great variety existed, were distinct from the Old Believers. The most numerous group was that of the Molokans, who derived their name from the practice of drinking milk (*moloko*) during fasts, by contrast with Orthodox Christians. They had over a million members at the beginning of the twentieth century – a sober, prosperous community, living mainly in the Caucasus, and basing its teaching on the Bible and the example of the early apostolic church. Members of another sect, the Dukhobors, emigrated to Canada through Tolstoy's generosity in giving them the profits from his novel *Resurrection*. They thus became the one Russian sect better known abroad than in Russia itself, largely for their disobedience to civil authority and habit of removing their clothes in public. Other sects included the Flagellants or Khlysty – probably a popular corruption of *Khristy* (Christs), the name by which the men referred to each other. They were less given to flagellation than to dancing provocative of religious ecstasy. They danced with a rotary motion, whereas others, the Jumpers (*skakuny*), bobbed up and down. In the more enthusiastic gatherings such episodes might end in sexual orgies, as is illustrated in Chekhov's *Murder* (1895). At the other extreme were the Eunuchs (*skoptsy*), who practised a custom which at least restricted their numbers – that of undergoing castration.

In the 1860s a Russian evangelical movement arose in the Ukraine, the Caucasus and St Petersburg. This began as a movement called Shtundism under the influence of German colonists in the Ukraine and of their Lutheran and Mennonite pastors. Evangelicism also made headway in St Petersburg's aristocratic circles, influenced by an Englishman, Lord Redstock, and an anglicised German, Dr Friedrich Baedeker. Dostoyevsky mentions Redstock in his *Diary of a Writer* for March 1876, and an evangelist portrayed in *Resurrection* was suggested to Tolstoy by Baedeker. The Union of Russian Baptists was founded in the Ukraine in 1884, but remained illegal until 1905, when a period of greater religious tolerance began.

Non-Russian citizens were the chief beneficiaries of the considerable tolerance extended in certain areas of religious activity. For example, Roman Catholics on Russian soil could usually find a place of worship. 'Throughout European Russia ... there was hardly a large town without its Catholic church or chapel' (Kolarz, p. 180). Catholic churches were also to be found in Siberia and Central Asia – in Tashkent, Tomsk, Tobolsk, Irkutsk and Vladivostok. These were built for Catholic Poles, Lithuanians and others – not for the Empire's Russian citizens. These were the main targets for religious persecution, since a Russian was expected to be Orthodox, leaving the more outlandish creeds to his alien compatriots. Missionary work by the Orthodox Church was accordingly encouraged, while proselytising by non-Orthodox persuasions was forbidden in law.

One consequence of Orthodox subservience to the government was that politically disaffected intellectuals tended to be anti-clerical, church and state being lumped together in their minds as equally pernicious.

12 Towns

GROWTH OF URBAN POPULATION   Though most Russians were countrymen, the population of the towns was growing fast in the eighteenth and nineteenth centuries – more than six times as rapidly as that of the countryside. The following figures show the increase (Kovalevsky, p. 60):

Year	Number of town-dwellers	Percentage of whole population
1812	1,653,000	4·4
1835	3,025,000	5·8
1851	3,482,000	7·8
1867	8,157,000	10·6
1897	16,785,212	13·0

There were few large towns. In 1867 only four cities in the Empire had a population of over one hundred thousand (St Petersburg, Moscow, Warsaw and Odessa), and even then one of those was Polish. By 1897 the number of such towns had risen to nineteen. They were, in descending order of size, St Petersburg, Moscow, Warsaw, Odessa, Lodz, Riga, Kiev, Kharkov, Tiflis, Vilna, Tashkent, Saratov, Kazan, Yekaterinoslav (now Dnepropetrovsk), Rostov-on-Don, Astrakhan, Baku, Tula and Kishinyov. Less than half of these towns were situated in Great Russian territory, and in several of them Russians figured only as a small minority.

APPEARANCE AND GENERAL ATMOSPHERE   Observers from western Europe hardly recognised Russian towns as towns. Less tactful foreigners, and some Russians too, described Moscow itself or even the whole Empire as one vast village. Observers also noted a lack of variety in Russian towns. Ample space and danger of fire encouraged a tendency to sprawl, and the wide streets were often unpaved, as in the villages. Paved roads, sewage systems, street lighting and piped water were not unheard of, but even by the beginning of the twentieth century they were still restricted to small, prosperous sections of the larger towns.

Most houses were single-storeyed and made of wood, but stone-built apartment houses of several storeys were also constructed in the towns where population pressure was greatest. It was common practice to rent apartments and houses rather than to own them, and the more salubrious might be occupied by wealthy officials, while the very poorest citizens resorted to some unsavoury doss-house. That of Khitrov Market in Moscow was a notorious haunt of tramps, prostitutes and thieves. Here professional beggar-women could hire emaciated babies to attract alms from passers-by, and if the child died in the course of the day so much the better, as this might elicit larger donations (Troyat, p. 61).

Despite such sinister examples of private enterprise the general atmosphere of Russian towns was torpid. There were few shops as understood in western Europe, shopping often being done in markets consisting of small, ill-lit stores, each exactly like its neighbour – the 'trading rows'. As in some villages, churches with painted domes might supply variety to the eye. In provincial capitals the governor's residence, court of justice, administrative offices, gymnasiums (grammar schools), hospitals and theatres provided a relatively imposing centre to the sprawling, ramshackle outskirts.

THE TWO CAPITALS   Two giants stood out among Russian towns and cities: the capital St Petersburg, and the old capital, Moscow. Both were well past the million mark in 1897, when St Petersburg had 1,267,023 inhabitants and Moscow 1,035, 664 – compare London, New York and Paris at the turn of the century, with 6,581,000, 3,437,000 and 2,660,000 respectively. Among Russian cities the nearest rival to St Petersburg and Moscow was Odessa with a mere 405,041 souls. The Tsars continued to be crowned in Moscow, and the habit of referring to St Petersburg and Moscow as the two capitals, even in official documents, showed that Russians had not forgotten where the seat of government had been before Peter the Great moved it in 1712.

The contrast between the two chief cities has frequently been emphasised. St Petersburg, Russia's 'window on Europe', was the more cosmopolitan, slick, fashionable and up-to-date. Its population included many government officials and foreigners, while its status as a port and the seat of the Russian court helped to make it magnificent and exotic. If St Petersburg called Moscow the largest village in the Empire, Muscovites could retort by claiming themselves more truly Russian. With its historical Kremlin and many churches or cathedrals ('forty times forty', according to legend), Moscow had a special hold on Russian affections. It was often called 'Mother' Moscow, an epithet comically inapplicable to the frigid and stately St Petersburg, which has the wrong grammatical gender in any case. But St Petersburg too had its affectionate nickname, *Piter*, deriving from the Dutch form of Peter the Great's name. Moscow was the headquarters of groups disapproving of Peter's reforming and europeanising activities – the slavophiles and the Old Believers, often considered the most Russian Russians. Herzen said that Petersburgers used to laugh at Muscovites' clothes, at their long hair and the shape of their whiskers. 'Moscow is a civilian city, rather dissolute, unused to discipline.' St Petersburg, by contrast, was like an army barracks. Everyone dressed identically. 'If you were to show an Englishman these battalions of tightly-buttoned fops in identical frock-coats on the Nevsky Prospekt [the city's most celebrated thoroughfare], he would think they were a squad of policemen' (*My Past and Thoughts*, ch. xxvi).

By the end of the century both capitals were centres of thriving industries. Moscow formed the core of the Central Industrial Region, devoted mainly to light industry and including the towns or industrial settlements of Tula, Yaroslavl, Orekhovo-Zuyevo, and Ivanovo-Voznesensk, 'the Russian Manchester'. St Petersburg was an important centre of the machine-tool industry. But it is not these aspects of the two capitals which are most richly illustrated by Russian literature.

The most celebrated invocation of the imperial capital, that in Pushkin's *Bronze Horseman* (written in 1833), is solemn and rhetorical, paying only passing attention to the capital's economic potentialities. The same author's *Eugene Onegin* begins and ends with the social whirl of St Petersburg, but also includes vivid pictures of the Russian countryside and of Muscovite society. Though Gogol began his career by describing Ukrainian rustics, some of his most notable work is found in his St Petersburg stories, of which the best-known are *The Nose* and *Nevsky Prospekt* (both 1835) and above all *The Overcoat* (1842). Dostoyevsky was brought up in Moscow. But he became an enthusiastic St Petersburger, and made the city a background for much of his early work describing the woes of petty officials and young men who rent miserable little rooms or screened-off corners of rooms in the slums. An impressive picture of the city from his mature period is that in *Crime and Punishment*, set near the picturesquely sordid Haymarket (*Sennaya ploshchad*).

Tolstoy differed from Dostoyevsky in finding country air sweeter than that of St Petersburg's tenements, but the two capitals figure as the background for much of *War and Peace* and *Anna Karenin*. It is fashionable city life which Tolstoy describes in his great novels – the world of counts, princes, hostesses, high officials and guards officers. Of the squalid side of city life he was, on his own confession, ignorant when he wrote *War and Peace* and *Anna Karenin*, for in his later *What then Must we Do?* (completed in 1886) he states: 'I had spent my life in the country and when I came to live in Moscow in 1881 the sight of urban poverty surprised me.' In this work Tolstoy describes the disturbing impression made by Moscow doss-houses, the Lyapin and Rzhanov Hostels, which he visited after volunteering to help to collect statistics for the census of 1882.

PROVINCIAL TOWNS Russian novelists tended to avoid identifying the provincial towns which frequently form the setting in their work, preferring to call them 'the town of N.' (or any other letter of the alphabet). Alternatively, such places may – like the setting of Dostoyevsky's *Devils* and the town in Chekhov's *My Life* – be called simply 'our town'. The identity of the town which forms the centre of Chichikov's intrigues in *Dead Souls* is concealed, but it was conceivably suggested to the author by Kursk. Similarly, the identity of the provincial capital in *Three Sisters* is not revealed in the text of the play, though Chekhov told Gorky that 'the action takes place in a provincial town such as Perm' (letter of 16 October 1900). The characteristic feature is that there were so many Kursks and Perms in Russia with little to differentiate one from the other. 'In Russia all towns are identical,' Chekhov once wrote. 'Yekaterinburg is just like Perm or Tula. It's also like Sumy and Gadyach' (letter of 29 April 1890). Even his home town Taganrog impressed Chekhov as boring, though it was no Sumy or Gadyach, but a port on the sea of Azov with a polyglot population of sailors and merchants, including

Greeks, Armenians and Bulgarians. It had a flourishing theatre and a public library – amenities by no means common in urban Russia – yet to Chekhov it was completely squalid, a place where people 'do nothing but eat, sleep and multiply and have no other interests' (letter of 7 April 1887). Chekhov's works abound in denunciations of provincial Russian towns such as that delivered by Andrew Prozorov in Act Four of *Three Sisters*. 'All these people do,' he says, repeating a familiar Chekhovian motif, 'is eat, drink and sleep till they drop down dead.' Another such diatribe appears in Chekhov's *My Life*:

> What kept these sixty-five thousand people going? That's what I couldn't see. Kimry got its living by boots, I knew. Tula made samovars and guns, Odessa was a port. But what our town was and what it did, I had no idea. Great Dvoryansky Street and a couple of the smarter streets were kept going on capital and civil servants' salaries paid by the government. But what of the other eight streets that ran parallel for a couple of miles and vanished behind the hill? What did they live on? That's what baffled me.
>
> The way these people lived was shameful beyond words. There was no park, no theatre, no decent orchestra. No one went inside the town library or club reading-room except for a few Jewish youths, so magazines and new books lay around uncut for months. Well-off professional people slept in cramped, stuffy bedrooms on wooden, bug-infested beds. They kept their children in revoltingly dirty rooms called nurseries, and servants, even old and respected ones, slept on the kitchen floor under rags. On fast-days their houses smelled of sturgeon fried in sunflower oil and on other days of borshch. Their food tasted awful and their drinking-water was unwholesome. At the town hall, governor's office, bishop's palace and all over town they had been going on for years about how we had no good, cheap water and must borrow two hundred thousand roubles from the government to lay on a proper supply. Very rich people – our town had about three dozen, who were known to gamble away whole estates at cards – also drank tainted water and talked excitedly about this loan, in fact they never stopped. It made no sense to me. I should have thought they would have found it easier to go ahead and put up the two hundred thousand out of their own pockets.
>
> I did not know one honest man in the whole town.
>
> My father took bribes, thinking they were offered out of respect for his moral calibre. And if boys wanted to be moved into a higher form at school they boarded out with their teachers and paid through the nose. At recruiting time the military commander's wife took bribes

from the young men. She was not above accepting a few drinks either, and was once too drunk to get off her knees in church. The doctors also took bribes at call-up time. The town medical officer and the vet levied a regular tax on butchers' shops and restaurants, and at the local college there was a brisk trade in certificates granting exemption from military service. The higher clergy took bribes from the lower and from churchwardens. If you applied to the municipal offices, the citizens' bureau, the health centre or any other institution they would shout after you, 'Remember to say thank you', and you would go back and hand over thirty or forty copecks.

SOCIAL COMPOSITION   By contrast with western Europe, where urbanisation has often been a more organic process, Russian towns tended to be artificial by-products of administrative policy. Catherine the Great set up over two hundred towns in just over twenty years, being persuaded that Russia required a *bourgeoisie* such as it clearly did not possess, but mainly in order to strengthen administrative control over her far-flung Empire. It was easy to create a town by decree. 'To transform a village into a town, it was necessary merely to prepare an *izba*, or log-house, for the district court, another for the police-office, a third for the prison, and so on.... All this required very little creative effort' (Mackenzie Wallace, i, p. 261). A hundred years after Catherine's death a Russian *bourgeoisie* had indeed come into being, and the usual claim that it was not very numerous is belied by statistics, since about half the urban population consisted of burghers, merchants and members of other bourgeois categories. But it is true that this was not a *bourgeoisie* on the European model and that it was not influential in affairs of state.

As already pointed out, many town-dwellers were peasants temporarily or permanently absent from their villages. Members of the non-landowning gentry also tended to reside in towns, while landowners often wintered in town, spending only part of the year on their estates. According to the 1897 census the peasants accounted for 38·8 per cent and the gentry for 6·2 per cent of all town-dwellers (Aleksandrov, p. 326). Most of the remainder, 44·3 per cent of the over-all urban population, belonged to the estate of the burghers. Though no better translation of the word *meshchanin* suggests itself, it must be added that 'burgher' conveys too solid an impression for a group which excluded merchants, a more prosperous category, and included small traders, owners of apartment-houses, craftsmen, factory workers and many others who could not be accommodated elsewhere. The burghers had their own communes with elected elders – less vital institutions than the village commune, but by no means ornamental, since they too could exile offending members to Siberia.

INDUSTRIAL WORKERS   By the end of the century the connection between the Russian factory worker and the village commune, with which he might still be registered, had grown tenuous. An increasing number of skilled workers were now second-generation proletarians. The number of factory workers as a whole may have reached three million by 1900 (see p. 64). Labour conditions were lamentably typical of industrial revolutions in general. Long hours, inadequate and irregular wages, sometimes compulsorily in kind (the so-called 'truck system') at disadvantageous terms from the factory shop, harsh fines for misdemeanours real or fancied, widespread use of child and female labour, inadequate safety precautions – all these were features of the Russian factory. So too were deplorable living conditions in shanty suburbs, or in the factory barracks where several families were sometimes crowded into one room, though at least such factory accommodation was usually free. Labour laws, for example those of 1882 and 1897, were passed in an attempt to improve these conditions – by provisions which were, however, often evaded. Trade unions were made illegal under a law of 1874, though in 1902 a high official of the Moscow police, Sergey Zubatov, founded a special workers' society with activities which included singing patriotic songs and demonstrating in favour of the Tsar. His purpose was to improve the workers' lot by non-revolutionary means. Russian workers went on strike many times in the last decades of the century, despite the suppression of unrest by police and mounted Cossacks, and labour troubles reached their most violent pre-1917 peak in the first Russian revolution, that of 1905.

All this is of historical importance, but the Russian industrial worker does not figure prominently in literature of the great age, partly because the great age was nearly over before the Russian worker came into any prominence. Chekhov was aware of the factory workers' miseries, as is shown in his story *A Case History* (1898) and elsewhere, but had no intimate knowledge of their life. He therefore showed these conditions only from outside, by contrast with his detailed pictures of the urban middle class and of rural Russia.

Among leading Russian writers Maxim Gorky was most closely acquainted with the urban poor – in fact it was he who popularised the Russian proletariat as a literary theme. But it was not so much factory workers as tramps and petty criminals, for example in the story *Chelkash* (1895) and the play *The Lower Depths*, who were his first main heroes. His story *Twenty-six Men and a Girl* (1899) portrays sweated workers in a small bakery. His most celebrated treatment of the factory worker proper is found in his novel *The Mother* (1907), which describes the Russian revolutionary movement, the action being based on the history of Sormovo, a district of Nizhny Novgorod (the author's home town, now renamed Gorky in his honour).

MERCHANTS AND BUSINESSMEN   Gorky's fiction takes in a wide social spectrum, and he has also described the urban *bourgeoisie*. Some of his studies of Russian merchants, including *The Arta-monovs' Business*, were, like *The Mother*, published outside the period considered here, but one of the best, *Foma Gordeyev* (1899), was his first novel and describes the wealthy merchant milieu on the Volga.

The merchants (*kuptsy*) formed a special class within Russian society. Since they included factory-owners as well as traders the term merchant may be misleading and it might be preferable to call them businessmen. Merchants did not form an estate in the same sense as the gentry and clergy, since the status of merchant was more precarious. It was not hereditary, but was obtained by paying the dues required to join one of the two (before 1863 three) merchants' Guilds, of which the First Guild was for the wealthier, including those engaged in foreign trade, while the Second was for humbler operators. At the beginning of the twentieth century the First Merchant Guild numbered 30,000 members and the Second about 400,000. If a merchant was unable to meet his dues he was likely to subside to the grade of burgher or peasant.

In contrast to the gentry and officials, merchants belonged (with the clergy and peasantry) to the less europeanised part of the community. They often wore huge beards and had their hair parted in the middle. The more old-fashioned wore long, black, double-breasted coats buttoned down the middle in traditional Russian style, whereas gentlemen dressed in the European manner. Merchants did not usually speak any language except Russian. They might even be unable to read or write, but to assume that such illiterates were poor businessmen could be an expensive mistake. Many successful merchants were Old Believers, and also clung to the ways of old Moscow by keeping their wives and daughters in comparative seclusion. They liked to dispense sturgeon and champagne at lavish banquets, where the presence of some 'Excellency' – a high official or general – was much prized as lending tone. Successful merchants built elaborately appointed houses with grand pianos which were never played, vast, ornate mirrors and other costly furniture. But such things were for show. When not entertaining, the host and his family might occupy poky little rooms in a less pretentious part of their home.

Merchants do not figure prominently in the works of Russian literature best known to foreign readers. But Lopakhin in Chekhov's *Cherry Orchard* is familiar to the world's theatre-goers, and a fuller study of the merchant milieu by the same author may be found in his story *Three Years* (1895). The main exploiter of merchants as a literary theme is a playwright little known outside Russia – Alexander Ostrovsky. Merchants also figure prominently in the gallery of Old Believer characters displayed in Melnikov-Pechersky's works. The industrialists of the Urals are described in the works of D.N. Mamin-Sibiryak, including his novel *The Privalov Millions* (1883).

OTHER CATEGORIES OF TOWN-DWELLERS   In addition to burghers and merchants the general category of town-dwellers included further subdivisions with smaller membership. These were honorary citizens, who might have either hereditary or life status. To this group were assigned for example sons of the clergy who had not entered the church, certain officials, and merchants who had made outstanding gifts to charity. The grade of honorary citizen was introduced in 1832 and was 'privileged' – that is, it conferred exemption from corporal punishment, recruitment and the poll-tax. Yet another estate, which existed in some towns, was constituted by the craft corporations (*tsekhi*). By the end of the nineteenth century, however, formal distinctions between all the estates were breaking down, and an individual might even not know his own social status until he needed a passport. As this suggests, Russian society was proceeding in the direction taken by western Europe – that of levelling out social distinctions.

LEISURE ACTIVITIES   In the disposal of leisure time town-dwellers did not follow the ritual of the countryside, though the church's influence was almost as strong in small towns as in the villages. Townsmen's opportunities for entertainment were naturally greater, and in the larger cities there were concerts and theatres to be visited. Picnics were a favourite amusement, especially if combined with gathering mushrooms. Muscovites, for example, could drive out to Sokolniki in the north-east of the city, where for a few copecks they could have the use of a ready-stoked samovar with which to make tea in the open air, while St Petersburgers could make excursions to the islands or the Gulf of Finland. Country picnics also offered revolutionaries the opportunity to conspire without being overheard by agents of the secret police.

Town parks provided bands and a pleasant place to dance or stroll in the evening. There were bazaars such as Moscow's mushroom bazaar, held in the first week of Lent on the ice of the Moscow River for the sale of dried and pickled mushrooms. It was also the practice to erect huge toboggan-slides in winter. Known, literally, as 'mountains', they descended from specially built towers. One of these was to be found in St Petersburg between the Alexander Column and the Admiralty, where it was possible to ascend again and proceed on a second slide to Dvortsovy Square. These huge slides were surrounded by trading and amusement booths. For those who found this tame, and could afford to indulge themselves, there were hectic rides in fast troikas with jingling bells, whipped along by *likhachi* (dare-devil drivers) to fashionable restaurants with champagne and choruses of gypsy girls. The dissolute customer might then move on 'somewhere else' (*yeshcho kuda-to*) – i.e. to a brothel. In keeping with the character of the two capitals, French or German restaurants predominated in St Petersburg, whereas Moscow's style was more national and the *traktir* or Russian inn, complete with icon, was the characteristic hostelry.

Two further amenities enjoyed by town-dwellers, at least of the more privileged sort, require comment. The first was the widespread use made of clubs. Some, such as the St Petersburg Yacht Club and English Club, were the exclusive meeting-place of diplomats, high officials and aristocrats. There were also commercial clubs for the use of merchants. Provincial centres all possessed their gentry clubs and there were often clubs for professional people, small officials and merchants. Clubs might contain a restaurant, a reading-room and a large hall for staging elaborate receptions and balls – such as that which takes place in the provincial gentry assembly hall in Chekhov's *Order of St Anne* (1895). But the main activity, according to literary and other evidence, was gambling over the card-table – often regarded as the main vice of the Russian privileged classes.

Another characteristic practice was that of hiring country cottages (*dachi*) not far from one's place of residence and preferably on a lake, river or sea accessible by railway. Urban husbands would establish their wives and children in such resorts for the summer, either remaining in town themselves or commuting to their place of work at seasonal reduced fares. The *dacha* husband, a joke figure as one particularly vulnerable to cuckolding, became a staple feature in *fin-de-siècle* anecdotes.

One custom not exclusive to Russian society was to keep open house at a fixed time each week, when it was possible for acquaintances to call informally. Hence such information as 'we receive on Thursdays', sometimes dispensed in Russian novels by the lady of the house, who usually took the leading role on social occasions. Such was the practice of polite society, but Russians of all classes were celebrated for their hospitality, which erred if at all by its very excess. The celebration of name-days and birthdays was one pleasant excuse for dispensing good cheer and another practice confined to urban Russia – as opposed to the village, where it was not much followed.

A corrective to any unduly rosy impression of nineteenth-century Russian urban life is provided in much of Gorky's fiction and in such earlier works as Gleb Uspensky's *Manners of Rasteryayev Street* (1866) describing the seamy side of his native Tula.

Part Four
LAW AND DISORDER

13 Officials

THE SYSTEM OF CONTROL   Imperial authority was enforced by a complex system of pressures and controls, some of which have already been indicated – the use made of the landowning gentry to keep the peasantry in subjection, and also of the Orthodox Church, conceived as a bulwark of the state and custodian of its ideology. The system of controls must now be further explored – the civil service, law-courts, press censorship, police and army, together with education, which the authorities attempted to exploit as a means of combating revolution and producing malleable citizens. Political opposition did, however, continue to flourish in the educational world, as in that of literature, while the zemstvos and law-courts also provided a forum for opponents of the governmental system.

Sporadically attacked from inside by enemies whom it could control but not eliminate, imperial Russia remained, on the whole, an effectively functioning society, even if its progress was halting and often unimpressive. How it worked is the concern of the present chapter, with particular reference to the civil service.

VARIETY OF OFFICIALS   Foreign visitors were often struck by the large number of officials who seemed to be everywhere in imperial Russia, all wearing uniform, with dark green the dominant colour. Besides civil servants they included many persons who would not automatically be regarded as functionaries in other societies, but who held official rank in Russia, and wore uniforms. Members of the liberal professions were often employed by the state, and many lawyers, doctors and architects accordingly held official rank. So too did university professors, who, if sufficiently distinguished, might rate the title 'Your Excellency', as does Professor Serebryakov in Chekhov's *Uncle Vanya*. Gymnasium (grammar-school) masters, being state employees, also rated as officials, for which reason a

schoolmaster such as Kulygin in Chekhov's *Three Sisters* may
appear on stage in uniform and even introduce himself as a 'court
councillor' (see p. 131).Students – for example Trofimov in Chekhov's *Cherry Orchard* – also wore a special uniform, though this provision was not in force throughout the period. Even merchants
might invent uniforms to enhance their importance in the world's
eyes.

The notion that every other Russian was an official is, therefore,
an exaggeration deriving partly from the national love of uniforms,
and from the fact that their wearers were naturally most numerous
in the two capitals, where foreigners were likely to notice them. The
actual ratio of civil servants to the population was, in the mid-nineteenth century, only twelve (roughly) to ten thousand of the population: a proportion three to four times lower than that prevailing
in western Europe at the time (Pipes, p. 281).

OFFICIALS AS SEEN IN LITERATURE The imperial word for
official, *chinovnik*, has become a term of abuse in Soviet Russia. That
this use of the word is justified is suggested by the evidence of nineteenth-century literature, since so many authors portray the workings of the bureaucracy as an indecorous farce. The first writer of
note to explore the theme was Gogol, himself briefly an official in
St Petersburg. He contributed two memorable studies – one comic,
the play *The Inspector-General*, and the other tragi-comic, *The
Overcoat*. Among many followers of Gogol the young Dostoyevsky
took up the theme with the downtrodden Makar Devushkin, hero
of his first novel, *Poor Folk*, and with the fantastic twin heroes of
his second novel, *The Double*.

Civil servants of the first four ranks were commonly called
'generals', though they might never have worn military uniform in
their lives. Civil service generals abound in Russian literature – so
much so that Virginia Woolf once claimed that, in a typical Russian
novel, 'we open the door and find ourselves in a room full of Russian
Generals' (Woolf p. 177). They were often comic figures – for
example, Dostoyevsky's *Nasty Anecdote* (1862) has a General Pra-
linsky, who intrudes on the wedding celebrations of a subordinate,
becomes helplessly drunk, collapses face down in a plate of blanc-
mange and has to be put to bed on the nuptial couch. As this episode
indicates, authors did not always defer to rank when ridiculing the
civil service, though by common consent a fairly low grade, that

of titular councillor (class nine), was the most ludicrous of all. The mere mention of a titular councillor was enough to create pleasurable tension in the reader, who could assume that slapstick comedy was likely to follow.

Should we then dismiss imperial officials as a mere absurdity? Herzen, who knew the milieu well, having himself been employed as a provincial official during exile to Vyatka and Novgorod, most emphatically did not think so. He explicitly dissociates himself from Gogol's exuberant ridicule in the following passage:

> One of the saddest results of Peter the Great's reforms is the development of officialdom. It is an artificial, uneducated, voracious class. Totally incompetent . . . and wholly ignorant of all except official forms, it is a sort of lay priesthood officiating in the law-courts and the police, and sucking the people's blood with thousands of thirsty and dirty mouths.

Gogol slightly raised one part of the curtain and showed us Russian officialdom in all its ugliness, but Gogol unintentionally reconciles us by making us laugh. His great comic talent overcomes his indignation. Besides, being shackled by Russian censorship, he could barely touch on the gloomy aspect of the squalid underworld in which the fates of the wretched Russian people are decided.

Somewhere in those smoke-stained offices through which we hustle, shabby persons are scribbling away on grey paper, then copying on to official stamped paper – and individuals, families and whole villages are injured, terrorised and ruined. A father goes into exile, a mother to prison and a son into the army, and it all bursts on them unexpectedly as a clap of thunder (*My Past and Thoughts*, ch. xv).

One unsavoury practice of provincial officials was to blackmail and terrorise vulnerable groups – minority peoples (especially Jews), Old Believers and sectarians – who were the victims of legal discrimination. Here the discretion permitted to local officials in interpreting complex and self-contradicting regulations could be a powerful weapon of extortion.

As Herzen's denunciation of the bureaucracy reminds us, not all officials in leading works of nineteenth-century fiction are ludicrous. For example, Anna Karenin's husband is an impressively serious study of a former provincial governor occupying a senior post in St Petersburg. Tolstoy clearly disapproves of Karenin and his activities, both official and unofficial, but treats him with respect – even though his sticking-out ears, pedantic manner, habit of cracking his fingers and false jocularity seem expressly created to antagonise his young son and drive his attractive wife to adultery. In his later novel *Resurrection*, Tolstoy portrays the higher bureaucracy even more unsympathetically, but makes his officials seem dangerous and heartless rather than ridiculous. Other serious studies of officials include Kalinovich, hero of Pisemsky's *A Thousand Souls*, whose rake's progress includes a period as a provincial governor. There is also an excellent portrait of a St Petersburg official – the dry, ironical, card-playing Orlov – in Chekhov's *Anonymous Story* (1893).

No author paid less respect to Herzen's protests against bureaucrat-baiting than Saltykov-Shchedrin, that supreme satirist of Russian officialdom. He was an official himself for a far longer period than Gogol or Herzen, rising to a provincial vice-governorship, and accordingly knew his subject exceptionally well. Among his many studies of preposterous officials his *History of a Certain Town* (1869–70) is outstanding. It describes a series of ridiculous governors, and the imaginary town Glupov (from *glupy*, 'stupid') becomes a potent symbol for the imperial administration as a whole.

Among the points scored against officials in literature, sycophancy towards those of higher rank, as in Chekhov's early *Fat and Thin* (1883), is prominent. But the most common accusation is that of taking bribes. As Chekhov stated in his devastating description, quoted in the previous chapter, of the unnamed provincial capital in *My Life*: 'If you applied to the municipal offices ... the health centre or any other institution they would shout after you, "Remember to say thank you", and you would go back and hand over thirty or forty copecks.' It has been argued in defence of these exactions that civil servants were badly paid and that bribery, almost in accordance with a fixed tariff, had become a traditional device for supplementing inadequate incomes. The dishonest official was not he who took bribes (since that was normal and respectable), but he who accepted a bribe when he could not perform the service for which it had been paid, or whose rapacity exceeded the agreed measure. One of Gogol's officials, for example, is accused of taking bribes 'above his station'.

RANKS, HONORIFICS AND AWARDS   The official class was a creation of Peter the Great. In 1722 he set up the celebrated hierarchy of fourteen grades, termed the table of ranks, which remained in force with few alterations until 1917. The ranks had cumbrous titles borrowed from Prussian and other western European models, and care is needed in translating them from Russian. 'Privy councillor' is, for example, a tempting rendering for *tayny sovetnik*, and is in fact adopted below for want of a better alternative, but can give a misleading impression in English. The fourteen ranks were as follows:

Class	Civilian Rank	Military Equivalent (after 1884)
1	Chancellor	Field Marshal
2	Actual Privy Councillor	General
3	Privy Councillor	Lieutenant-General
4	Actual State Councillor	Major-General
5	State Councillor	
6	Collegiate Councillor	Colonel
7	Court Councillor	Lieutenant-Colonel
8	Collegiate Assessor	Captain
9	Titular Councillor	Staff Captain
10	Collegiate Secretary	Lieutenant
11	Ship's Secretary	
12	Provincial (*gubernsky*) Secretary	Sub-Lieutenant
13	Provincial (*provintsialny*) Secretary	
14	Collegiate Registrar	

Of the above, classes eleven and thirteen fell into abeyance in the first half of the nineteenth century, and the military rank of major, formerly the equivalent of collegiate assessor, was discontinued in 1884.

Each official had an honorific title with which he was addressed by subordinates and on official occasions. Classes one and two above were 'Your Supreme Excellency'; three, four and five rated as 'Your Excellency'; six to eight inclusive were 'Your Supreme Honour' and the remainder 'Your Honour'. Wives were also entitled to these honorifics, whence the occasions on which Anna Karenin is referred to as Her Excellency.

Officials were periodically awarded decorations called 'orders'. Most of these had several grades, like that of St Vladimir with its four classes, even the lowest of which (class four) conferred hereditary membership of the gentry on the recipient. The order of St Anne (with three classes) was less exalted – after receiving his St Anne (class two), the hero of Chekhov's *Order of St Anne* planned to move on to the St Vladimir ladder and was rash enough to hint as much by making an execrable pun to the local provincial governor when, in accordance with etiquette, he paid a call to thank His Excellency for the award. Other orders included the four classes of the military order of St George, conferred for outstanding bravery, and the orders of St Stanislaus (three classes), which formed the humblest category of those granted to civilians. Less commonly encountered in literature are: the order of St Andrew (one class only), given to members of the imperial family and the highest of the orders; the order of the White Eagle (one class); of Alexander Nevsky (one class); and of St Catherine (for women, two classes).

HIGHER GOVERNMENTAL ORGANS   As already indicated, even the most exalted governmental organs had the function of executing the sovereign's will rather than of initiating policy. This is true of four bodies which must now be mentioned. The Senate had originally been established by Peter the Great in 1711 to supervise the entire administration and as the chief legislative, administrative and judicial organ. Its powers fell far short of this in practice, especially in the period studied here, having decreased notably in the 1810s with the institution of the ministries (which were formally subordinate to it) and of the Committee of Ministers. From 1864 onwards, however, the Senate at least operated as a court of appeal, besides discharging numerous minor functions. The Committee of Ministers functioned from 1802 to 1906 with the task of co-ordinating the work of different departments. Its capacity was mainly advisory, as was that of the Council of State, set up in 1810 to discuss, but not to initiate, legislation. A similar role was fulfilled by a shorter-lived body, the Council of Ministers, which met at the Tsar's discretion and under his presidency between 1861 and 1882.

The ministries, establishment of which was completed in 1811, played an important part in the administration. They have been described as 'state departments of the usual west-European type, each with a well-defined competence and each under the direction of a minister who was personally responsible for the legality of his actions' (Karpovich, p. 18). To this must be added a reminder that ministers were appointed and dismissed as the Tsar saw fit, and that he could take their advice or not as he wished.

The following ministries were functioning at the end of the nineteenth century: foreign affairs; war; internal affairs; justice;

finance; agriculture and state properties; transport; education. To these eight must be added the administration of state horse-breeding, and a body called state control, responsible for auditing government income and expenditure. Though the ministries were all subordinated to the Senate and department of state control, there were also numerous bodies directly responsible to the Tsar: the ministry of the imperial court; his Majesty's personal Chancery: his Majesty's personal chancery for the institutes of the Empress Mariya (responsible for orphanages and girls' schools). There was also an imperial chancery for dealing with petitions.

The ministries maintained staffs of varying size and structure, according to their own particular needs, in the provinces as well as in St Petersburg. For instance, the provincial gendarmerie or security police (after 1880), together with provincial postal, telegraph and censorship officials, came under the ministry for internal affairs, and the ministry of finance maintained provincial offices for tax-collecting purposes. Other ministries too had sizeable provincial establishments.

PROVINCIAL ADMINISTRATION As representatives of central government, provincial governors exercised general supervision over all local officials and were more directly responsible for some in their capacity as representatives of the ministry of internal affairs. The provinces were, accordingly, by no means starved of bureaucrats, as the many works of literature devoted to provincial officialdom illustrate.

For administrative purposes the Empire was divided into territorial units, of which there were one hundred and one at the end of the nineteenth century. They consisted chiefly of the provinces (*gubernii*), of which there were seventy-eight and of regions (*oblasti*), of which there were eighteen and which may be considered provinces under a different name – they were in fact areas remote from the centre or possessing unusual social institutions. Provinces and regions differed greatly in size and density of population, their average area being greater than that of Belgium. The population varied from a few hundred thousand to just over four million, some of the largest in area being the least populous. The vast, sparsely inhabited Yakutsk Region in eastern Siberia (with a population of just under three hundred thousand at the end of the nineteenth century) may be contrasted with Kiev Province – covering only one eightieth

5 *Russia in Europe:* administrative boundaries (late nineteenth century). Where the name of a town is underlined, it is the same name as the province or region of which it is the capital. Thus <u>Tambov</u> is the capital of Tambov Province. The administrative areas are smaller than those of Russia in Asia because of European Russia's greater population density.

of the area of the Yakutsk Region, it yet boasted a population four-teen times as great.

Each province and region came under the administrative control of a governor appointed by the central government, and resident in the provincial capital (*gubernsky gorod*), which usually gave its name to the province as a whole – thus: Tula Province, Vladimir Province. But some provinces, for instance Podolia and Volhynia, had names not deriving from those of their chief towns. Provinces were subdivided into smaller units termed districts (*uyezdy*), each with a district capital (*uyezdny gorod*) as its administrative centre. There were about eight districts within a typical province. Districts did not have governors, but came under the administrative control of their chief of police, the so-called *ispravnik*.

In some areas several provinces or regions were grouped together in general-governorships, under governor-generals, who, as the name implies, exercised military as well as civil authority. There were nine such general-governorships at the end of the nineteenth century – all on the periphery of the Empire, mainly in areas requir-ing a swifter reaction to potential crises than could be mobilised by the distant central authority: Finland; the Kingdom of Poland; the Caucasus; (in European Russia) the South-West and North-West Territories; (in Siberia) Irkutsk and Amur; (in Central Asia) Turkestan and the Steppe. The city of Moscow also had a governor-general – a compliment to its status as the old capital.

Four city administrations were directly responsible to the central government: those of St Petersburg, Odessa, Sevastopol and Kerch-Yenikale, each of which came under a town captain (*gradona-chalnik*). To complete the tally, the island and penal settlement of Sakhalin enjoyed the status of department (*otdel*).

LOCAL GOVERNMENT   It will be remembered that the reforms of Alexander II included provisions for a new kind of local govern-ment, that of the zemstvos (rural councils) instituted by a law of 1864, and also of town councils (*gorodskiye dumy*) instituted by a law of 1870. These bodies were elective, albeit on a complex system with heavy weighting in favour of the gentry and of property owners. Zemstvos were established on both provincial and district levels, having their headquarters in provincial and district capitals. Their members, elected for periods of three years, in turn elected execu-tive boards, also for three years, to manage current business. Provincial councillors were elected by district councillors, and they also elected executive boards. The town councils had a similar organisation, being elected for four years and forming an executive board.

There thus arose, in sharp contrast to the traditional *chinovnik*, a new kind of official – welfare-minded, public-spirited and the repository of the hopes of Russian liberals, who saw in the new local-government institutions a school of practical democracy.

The rural councillors and officials often saw themselves in this light too – and so, unfortunately, did the central authority, which proceeded to hamper them in various ways. Zemstvos did not even operate in all provinces, for by the end of the century they were functioning in only thirty-four, besides which the 'counter-reforms' of Alexander III included a law of 1890 limiting their power and increasing their dependence on the state. They were in any case impeded by powers of near-veto conferred on provincial governors, by the ultimate control of the ministry of the interior and by the difficulty of levying taxes adequate to their requirements. They were also compelled to accept the local marshal of the gentry (of district or province as the case might be) as chairman – confirmation of the gentry's dominant position. Peasants did, however, find their way on to the councils – where they often showed themselves more conservative than the representatives of the gentry on whom the government relied to keep them under control.

The councils were largely concerned with local economic needs – upkeep of roads and bridges, anti-famine precautions, medical care and elementary schools. By the end of the century they were employing many teachers and doctors, among whom they attracted the more radical-minded. Attempts by the councils to exercise wider political influence, outside the confines of local affairs, were carefully watched and thwarted by central authority. A certain tension existed between the local councils with their new, progressive traditions, and the state officials, though the latter were by no means all the hidebound reactionaries of popular mythology.

14 Crime and punishment

JUDICIAL REFORM   The overhaul of the judicial system, enacted in 1864, is widely considered the most effective among Alexander II's many reforms. There was much room for improvement, since justice had previously been administered according to a complex and cumbrous system by judges dependent on the administration, badly paid and operating in secret at wearisome length, all evidence having to be taken down in writing. Class distinctions were also reflected in the treatment which a citizen might receive at the hands of the law. Writing in the period preceding the judicial reforms, Herzen stated:

> To know the real meaning of Russian prisons, courts and police, you have to be a peasant.... Political prisoners, who mostly belong to the gentry, are strictly confined and savagely punished, but their fate is not at all to be compared to that of the unhappy bearded ones [the peasants]. ... Such is the chaos, brutality, arbitrariness and perverseness of the Russian law-courts and police, that an ordinary person ... does not fear punishment so much as the process of the law. He waits impatiently to be sent to Siberia, his martyrdom ending with the beginning of his punishment.
>
> (*My Past and Thoughts*, ch. x.)

The new system introduced in 1864 was based largely on the French and to some extent on the English model. Procedure was simplified and made public. It was arranged for judges to receive adequate salaries and to hold their appointments permanently unless they themselves should be convicted of a crime. They thus became less dependent on the administration, though not entirely independent, for threats of transfer to a less attractive neighbourhood and other pressures could still be applied. Trial by jury was introduced for more serious criminal cases, and barristers – with

clearly defined qualifications and their own professional association – made their appearance. The new system operated under the
passive supervision of the Senate, which maintained cassation departments as courts of appeal empowered to order re-trial, and
under the more active supervision of the ministry of justice, which
had a representative, the public prosecutor, in each of the newly
constituted county courts (*okruzhnyye sudy*) to act as prosecuting
counsel in criminal trials.

The reformed courts became, as literature itself had become, an
outlet for freedom of speech otherwise denied public expression.
Russian advocates – for example, the public prosecutor at Dmitry
Karamazov's trial in *The Brothers Karamazov* – were often carried
away by eloquence on topics not relevant to the issues before the
court. Moreover, as Dostoyevsky often complains in his journalistic
articles, Russian juries were excessively tender-hearted, even going
so far as to acquit prisoners who had pleaded guilty. An instance
of this occurred in 1878 when a revolutionary, Vera Zasulich, was
acquitted by a jury after shooting and wounding General Trepov,
town captain of St Petersburg, who had ordered the flogging of a
political prisoner. The episode inspired Turgenev's *Threshold*, one
of his *Poems in Prose* (1879–83), in which he invokes a female revolutionary.

THE NEW COURTS   County courts were introduced gradually from
1866 onwards, and their jurisdiction normally extended over a province. Appeal from their decisions could be made in the first instance
to the appropriate chamber of justice (*sudebnaya palata*), with jurisdiction over several provinces. County courts and chambers of justice were for more serious offences. Minor matters (involving civil
disputes over a sum below five hundred roubles, and criminal cases
in which the penalty did not exceed a three-hundred-rouble fine
or one year's imprisonment) were to be adjudicated by justices of
the peace elected by district zemstvo assemblies. In these courts
the procedure was informal and fatherly – a contrast to the relative
pomp of the county court with its three uniformed judges (the presi-
dent in the centre) and barristers in frock-coats. From justices of
the peace appeal was made in the first instance to the district
assembly of justices of the peace. But the jurisdiction of justices
of the peace was much reduced in 1889 with the institution of land
captains, who took over their functions in the countryside. Moreover

town courts, with judges appointed by the ministry of justice – not elected, as were the justices of the peace – replaced them in many urban areas. By the beginning of the twentieth century the so-called peace courts were operating only in Moscow, St Petersburg and six other large towns.

After emancipation the peasants, some three quarters of the population, became (as stated above) subject to trial for minor offences by cantonal courts consisting of fellow-peasants, often illiterate. These enforced peasant law based on custom and dealt with petty theft, family disputes and so on. In addition to these, military courts judged offences committed by military personnel and also, as shown below, certain offences committed by civilians. Ecclesiastical courts tried divorce cases and those involving the discipline and professional interests of the clergy. There were also special commercial courts in certain cities of the Empire.

POLICE The governor of each province was also the head of the police within the province, and it will be remembered that at district level the chief of police, the *ispravnik*, was also head of the district administration as a whole. For police purposes districts were subdivided at the next level down into units called *stany*, each consisting of several cantons. The chief of police for a *stan* was the *stan* prefect (*stanovoy pristav*), below whom came a number of (usually) mounted policemen called *uryadniki* – the office was introduced in 1878 in order to quell increasing rural unrest. At the lowest level peasants termed 'hundredsmen' and 'tensmen', responsible to the *uryadnik*, were elected to discharge the most menial police duties, on a part-time basis, and the village elders also carried out certain quasi-police functions. Large towns had a different police organisation under special chiefs of police.

The above remarks apply to the ordinary police. There was also a special security or political police, distinguished by light blue uniforms: the gendarmerie. During the existence of the Third Section of the imperial chancery, from 1826 to 1880, the gendarmerie was controlled by the head of the Third Section, but after 1880 it was transferred to the ministry of the interior, which already controlled the ordinary police. Secret agents and *agents provocateurs* reinforced the work of the uniformed gendarmerie and had the task of penetrating revolutionary conspiracies – for the security apparatus as a whole the colloquial term *okhrana* ('protection') was often used. The gendarmerie was also responsible for policing the railways – hence the occasional presence of a gendarme on station platforms in Russian fiction.

Uniformed or secret, ordinary or political, policemen were mistrusted and despised by the average citizen – to an extent which the resourceful Mackenzie Wallace did not appreciate at the beginning of his investigations into nineteenth-century Russia. Having equipped himself with a document from the gendarmerie to certify that during his travels round Russia he was not engaged on any nefarious activity, he found that presentation of it only made him the object of immediate suspicion to any decent citizen (Mackenzie Wallace, i, pp. 318–19).

INVESTIGATION AND TRIAL   In 1860 the investigation of criminal cases was removed from the frequently brutal police and entrusted to 'judicial investigators' (*sudebnyye sledovateli*) – in effect, examining magistrates. These were nominally independent of police and public prosecutors, and were at first intended to enjoy permanent tenure of office. In practice, however, the ministry of justice found it prudent to appoint them on a temporary basis to make them more amenable. A memorable fictional investigator is to be found in Dostoyevsky's *Crime and Punishment* – Porfiry Petrovich, who uses 'psychological' methods to induce the murderer Raskolnikov to confess.

Dostoyevsky has also contributed the particularly detailed and fascinating fictional murder trial mentioned above – that of Dmitry Karamazov in *The Brothers Karamazov*. Notable too among literary trials is that of Catherine Maslov in Tolstoy's *Resurrection*, which begins when the prisoner is brought from gaol to face her judges in a county court. *Resurrection* provides an especially full picture of legal and penal procedure, including descriptions of the hearing of an appeal to the Senate, of prison conditions and of transportation to Siberia. The novel is set in the 1880s, by which time the 'new' courts were no longer so new, and Tolstoy's satirical description was a sharp corrective to any undue optimism about the reformed judiciary. Readers may also ponder the fact that Dmitry Karamazov and Catherine Maslov are both victims of a miscarriage of justice.

PENALTIES   Capital punishment was abolished in 1753, except for the murder or attempted murder of a member of the imperial family.

But this provision was sometimes evaded. It was possible to award so many strokes of the knout that death was likely to follow. The use of the knout was banned early in the reign of Nicholas I, and that of the birch by a law of 1863 abolishing the severest forms of corporal punishment. After this measure flogging could, however, be administered to delinquent peasants on the orders of cantonal courts. It could also be imposed in disciplinary units of the army, and on prisoners and deportees to Siberia, for disciplinary offences. With regard to political offenders, Vera Zasulich's acquittal (see p. 138) incensed the authorities, and henceforward care was taken to see that such cases did not come before juries. A special court had already been set up in St Petersburg in 1872 to try cases of treason, besides which wide use was made of powers of exile and other punishment by so-called administrative procedure – that is, without trial and on the decision of officials.

Military courts retained the power to impose capital punishment. Political conspirators and assassins, of whom there were so many in the last decades of the monarchy, accordingly became liable to execution. This was legalised by declaring throughout large areas of the Empire states of emergency whereby such offences were tried by military courts, and not by the ordinary courts which had no power to impose the death sentence.

It will be remembered that the Decembrist poet Ryleyev and Lenin's elder brother Alexander were among nineteenth-century Russians who were executed, and that Dostoyevsky narrowly escaped this fate, only to suffer a variety of other penalties. His *Memoirs from the House of the Dead*, in effect an account of his four years in gaol at Omsk in Siberia, is a classic of Russian penal literature and it is regrettable that he has not left as full an account of his months in the Fortress of St Peter and St Paul in St Petersburg before trial. On release from gaol, Dostoyevsky was compelled to serve as a private in an army unit, another common form of punishment, and was gradually permitted the privileges of promotion, demobilisation, residence in European Russia – and finally of residence in St Petersburg whence he had been deported ten years earlier.

As Dostoyevsky's penal history reminds us, fortresses and monasteries were available as places of incarceration in addition to ordinary prisons. The Fortress of St Peter and St Paul had an especially distinguished roll of nineteenth-century inmates, rivalled by that of Schlüsselburg Fortress, also on an island in the Neva. Monasteries conveniently equipped with dungeons included that on the remote Solovetsky Islands in the White Sea, and Suzdal Monastery, about a hundred and forty miles from Moscow.

Sentence to Siberia took two forms, of which the more severe was termed *katorga*, sometimes misleadingly translated 'hard labour'. Hard labour, for example in the notorious silver mines of Nerchinsk, might or might not be involved, but what *katorga* (originally denoting 'galley') specifically implied was confinement in a Siberian gaol with the status of convict. Even when the sentence had been served, compulsory permanent exile to Siberia followed. As a milder punishment, exile without convict status was commonly imposed on those termed 'exile-deportees' (*ssylno-pereselentsy*).

The impact of exile, usually less than that of *katorga*, yet offered a wide range of disquieting possibilities. Being confined temporarily to a family estate in European Russia, as happened to Turgenev and Pushkin, was the least uncomfortable form of banishment. In extreme cases an exile might languish under the eye of a local policeman somewhere in the Yakutsk Region. Hard though the life might be, such deportees (in the case of political prisoners) were usually members of the gentry with independent means, or were paid a small subsistence allowance by the government. They were often treated as social superiors by the local inhabitants, being free to receive and write books, and to correspond with friends. They might also be able to take their valets with them, as did Herzen when exiled to Perm and Vyatka.

Enormous distances and a harsh climate made escape from Siberia difficult, but the attempt was often successfully undertaken. Siberian peasants would leave food and drink outside their houses for the benefit of escapees. This was done partly through sympathy, for the common people thought of convicts as the 'unfortunate' or 'unlucky' ones, but was also a form of insurance, since such desperadoes were less likely to break into a hut if they could find food and drink outside it.

The number of persons imprisoned and exiled for political reasons seems insignificant if comparison is made with the scale of persecution operated by twentieth-century totalitarian states. Yet the victims' sufferings should not be underestimated. Arising more from gross administrative incompetence than from widespread and systematic brutality, these tribulations included extreme overcrowding in transit prisons, prison barges and permanent gaols together with stink, lice, bugs, cockroaches, epidemic disease and consequent high mortality. Convicts often had half their heads shaved. They wore ankle-fetters and a so-called 'dressing-gown' with a device on the back like an ace of diamonds. The political prisoners among them were kept under especially close supervision. Visiting the penal colony of Sakhalin in 1890, Chekhov was allowed free access to all prisoners except the 'politicals', and *Sakhalin Island* – his study of penal conditions based on these experiences – is an impressive work from both a scholarly and a literary point of view. As it reminds us, the imperial authorities did not hesitate to use the term 'political prisoners', for it was not then thought necessary, as in more recent times, to pretend that persons persecuted for political reasons had committed some non-political offence.

Whether in prison or exile, political offenders enjoyed considerable freedom to read and write. Chernyshevsky not only wrote *What is to be Done?* in the Fortress of St Peter and St Paul, but also did other writing and translation there and in Siberia. Pisarev spent four and a half years in the same fortress, producing his most influential work there. P.G. Zaichnevsky even composed the manifesto *Young Russia*, one of the most inflammatory clandestine revolutionary pamphlets of the 1860s, while in a Moscow gaol, where his cell became an informal discussion club for university students who came and went almost as they wished. There was at least one instance of an imprisoned revolutionary being permitted to leave his cell under a soldier's escort in order to buy political literature in a St Petersburg bookshop. It is not at all surprising to find Lenin completing his *Development of Capitalism in Russia*, and also indulging in extensive journalism, while exiled to southern Siberia between 1897 and 1900.

15 The army

IN POLITICAL AND SOCIAL LIFE   The armed forces were an important pillar of the imperial system, not least because of a tradition whereby army generals were frequently appointed to ministerial and other high civil offices. The army figures prominently in literature, Lermontov, Tolstoy and Dostoyevsky all having served as officers, though the last-named always remained one of nature's civilians. The imperial navy is less prominent in nineteenth-century literature, as it was in Russian life, but one important literary work is associated with it – Goncharov's *Frigate Pallas*, based on his experiences as civilian secretary to the governmental mission to Japan headed by Admiral Ye. V. Putyatin in 1852–4.

Though in many ways a backward and cruel institution in the early nineteenth century, the Russian army was not exclusively officered by diehard reactionaries. Only, perhaps, in a land of surprises such as imperial Russia might one find nineteenth-century guards officers in the vanguard of a movement for reform and revolution. Yet such a tradition was established during the period of subversive secret societies which flourished after the Napoleonic campaigns of 1812–15. These impressed the many Russian troops serving in western Europe with the backwardness of their own country, showing them that forms of government other than the autocratic existed elsewhere – an experience which helped to inspire the Decembrist revolt of 1825.

A Russian guards regiment, the Semyonovsky, had mutinied in 1820. Yet the guards were a social élite in Russia, as elsewhere, 'quite fit to be compared with the German in the social position of their officer corps' (Schlesinger, p. 361). But officers of less illustrious, non-guards regiments, normally dependent on their meagre pay, were comparatively humble individuals. One may contrast Lieutenant-Colonel Count Vronsky – lover of Anna Karenin, owner of race horses and vast estates – with the less resplendent Lieutenant-Colonel Vershinin, the battery commander in Chekhov's *Three Sisters*, who had an unpresentable wife with suicidal tendencies and spent all his life 'knocking around from one set of lodgings to another, with a couple of chairs and a sofa and stoves smoking all the time'.

IN LITERATURE   Pushkin's work includes descriptions of the Russian army in the late eighteenth century at the time of the Pugachov rebellion – *The Captain's Daughter* and *The History of the Pugachov Rebellion*. As mentioned above, his *Journey to Erzerum* describes his own adventures as camp-follower to the Russian army during war against the Turks in 1829. Lermontov went a stage further than the civilian Pushkin by obtaining a commission in the Hussars in 1834, and he made an army officer, Pechorin, the 'Hero of our Time' in his novel of that name. Dostoyevsky trained as a cadet and junior officer in a military engineering school and, though he quickly resigned his commission, was later compelled to serve with the army in Siberia as part of his punishment for political misdemeanours. He made little use of his army experiences in fiction, however.

Tolstoy, who saw active service as an officer, was more inclined to exploit the army as literary copy. His descriptions begin with early stories, *The Raid* (1853) and *The Wood-Felling* (1855), reflecting his experiences in the Russian army of the Caucasus in 1851–4. Tolstoy also saw active service at the siege of Sevastopol during the Crimean War, and made use of it in his *Sevastopol Stories* (1855–6). He later delved back into earlier martial history with his epic of the Napoleonic campaigns, *War and Peace*.

Duels fought in defence of marital or regimental honour, reckless gambling, exciting love affairs and alcoholic orgies are among the more romantic features of the Russian officer's daily round, as portrayed in nineteenth-century fiction. There was, however, another aspect to military life, as Tolstoy himself did not conceal. For an account more concentrated on the indecorous side of the Mess and less likely to stimulate recruiting than Tolstoy's, readers could turn to Kuprin's *The Duel* (1905).

THE PRE-REFORM ARMY   Russian fiction about the army tends to ignore the 'other ranks', whose conditions of life, especially in the first part of the nineteenth century, were unenviable. Conscription was selective, but on a class basis, gentry and clergy being exempt, as also were merchants on payment of a special tax. Conscripts were accordingly drawn from the peasantry and from the lower ranks of townspeople – craftsmen and burghers. Young peasants dreaded the prospect of having 'their foreheads shaved', as happened to those unlucky enough to be selected as recruits. This was regarded as the prelude to a lingering death, owing to the harshness of conditions and to the fact that the term of service in the ranks was so long – normally twenty-five years until after the Crimean War, when it was reduced to fifteen, among other relaxations heralding the conscription law of 1874, described below. A soldier's wife became, in practice, almost a widow. And yet, despite all disadvantages, it was sometimes possible for a conscript to buy a substitute.

Disciplinary punishments were brutal. They included flogging and running the gauntlet, whereby the victim was dragged between ranks of fellow-soldiers compelled to beat him with switches of willow as he passed along the so-called 'green road'. The number of blows inflicted might run into several thousand. After the mutiny of 1831 at Staraya Russa in Novgorod Province – provoked by a rumour that soldiers were being deliberately infected with cholera by the authorities – a prolonged orgy of knoutings, floggings and beatings was ordered by Nicholas I, and led to well over a hundred deaths among some two thousand six hundred mutineers who were punished (Riasanovsky, *Nicholas I*, p. 14). Running the gauntlet, as still practised some twenty years later, is vividly described in Dostoyevsky's *Memoirs from the House of the Dead*.

REFORM   Conditions were greatly improved by the army reforms of General D.A. Milyutin, minister of war from 1861 to 1881. In the law of 1874 he removed class discrimination from conscription, to which every male citizen over the age of twenty-one now became liable, though it was not usually necessary to call up more than a third of them in peace time. Moreover, certain categories – including the clergy, only sons and men who had brothers with the colours – were exempt. The period of active service was reduced to six years followed by a number of years in the reserve and militia. Further concessions benefited those who had attended school and university. University students were liable to only six months with the colours, while ex-pupils of the gymnasiums and other secondary schools need serve only eighteen months or three years, and ex-pupils of primary schools need serve only four. For university and secondary school graduates who cared to enlist voluntarily rather than take their chance of not being conscripted, the above terms were halved.

Many peasants first learned to read and write in the reformed army, for Milyutin put military education on a sound footing. Discipline was considerably relaxed, corporal punishment being now confined, at least in theory, to penal units, though it was not uncommon, even after the reforms, for an officer to strike a soldier.

Conditions remained deplorable by absolute standards, but the situation had been transformed by Milyutin's reforms if comparison is made with the early years of the century.

Chekhov was sympathetically disposed towards the Russian army. According to Stanislavsky, he sent his own military representative to supervise the rehearsals of *Three Sisters*, in which army officers figure prominently. Chekhov required his officers to be played as 'charming, decent people', not as heel-clicking popinjays. If Stanislavsky is to be believed, Chekhov would also emphasise the cultural mission performed by the Russian army when posted to remote parts of the country, to which it took 'knowledge, art, happiness and joy' (*The Oxford Chekhov*, iii, pp. 314–16).

Like so much else in life, the Russian army had its good and bad sides. As befits the 'broad Russian nature', the interval between them was especially wide.

16 Education

GENERAL DEVELOPMENT The progress of nineteenth-century Russian education follows the pattern of imperial development in general by showing fairly impressive improvement on modest beginnings. Educational facilities had greatly expanded by the end of the century. For instance, in 1899 the Empire had nine universities with about 17,000 students, whereas there had been a mere 450 students in four universities in 1809 – a figure which does not include the non-Russian universities of Helsingfors and Vilna (Florinsky, ii, p. 726; Kovalevsky, p. 482). On the other hand, imperial education is less impressive if compared with that offered by the advanced countries of western Europe in the same period. An eloquent figure reflecting educational backwardness is the high proportion of citizens of the Empire between the ages of nine and forty-nine recorded as illiterate in the 1897 census: seventy-four per cent.

AUTHORS AS PUPILS The variety of Russian education is well illustrated by considering how certain leading writers fared in youth. Turgenev and Tolstoy were instructed at home by private tutors, as befitted these heirs of rich landowners, though Turgenev did briefly attend a preparatory school in Moscow and was taught to read Russian by an amateur, his father's valet. Wealthy gentry families such as these commonly employed resident tutors and governesses, who were often French, British or German, and were thus equipped to provide their charges with oral practice in foreign languages. In his *Childhood*, to some extent a fictional account of his own early years, Tolstoy describes a German tutor, Karl Ivanovich Mauer, who is modelled on his own real-life tutor, Theodor Rössel. Rössel was succeeded as Tolstoy's tutor by a Frenchman, St Thomas, who appears in *Childhood* under the name St Jérôme.

Turgenev and Tolstoy became university students aged fifteen

and sixteen respectively, for in the first half of the century the age
for entering the university was low by modern standards. Tolstoy
went to the University of Kazan, where he studied oriental languages for a year and then switched to jurisprudence, but failed to
take his degree. Turgenev attended three universities. He put in
one term at Moscow before going to St Petersburg, where he gradu-
ated in 1837 after three years in the history–philology faculty, then
attended the University of Berlin for a time, returning to St Petersburg to begin reading for an MA degree with which he did not persist.
All this, to which perhaps should be added his honorary degree at
Oxford (1879), makes Turgenev the most academically involved of
the great Russian writers, but not the most erudite – Tolstoy, who
pursued knowledge so devotedly in so many fields, surely deserves
that honour. Tolstoy also gave more attention than any other leading
Russian writer to the theory and practice of education itself.

Pushkin did not attend a university, but received the most exclusive of institutional upper-class educations available to Russian boys
at the Imperial Alexander Lycée at Tsarskoye Selo, the Tsar's residence near St Petersburg. He joined this establishment in the year
of its foundation, 1811, and left in 1817. This was a boarding-school
with a preliminary class and a six-year course, of which the first
three years provided general education and the last three a legal and
'political' training. The school was designed to produce high functionaries, but also became a nursery of poets, of whom Pushkin was
the most illustrious. He retained happy memories of his years at
the lycée, later commemorated in his lyrics. After leaving school
he became an official of the ministry of foreign affairs, but did not
last long in what was a most unexacting position.

Pushkin's near-contemporary Gogol also failed to attend university and also became an official in St Petersburg after leaving
his school – another well-known lycée, that of Nezhin in the Ukraine.
He had ambitions to shine as an administrator, but his civil-service
career was brief, as was his later tenure of a professorship at St
Petersburg University from 1834 to 1835. Turgenev was one of his
students and has described how the new professor missed two out
of every three lectures, spoke inaudibly, seemed highly embar-
rassed, and, when conducting the final oral examinations in his subject, sat with a handkerchief wrapped round his face and failed to
ask the candidates any questions.

Dostoyevsky had an education ill suited to his temperament.

After being a pupil of private schools in Moscow as a boy, he trained as a cadet at the Military Engineering School in St Petersburg, passing out in 1843 with an army commission which he resigned in the following year. He had combined military training with the wide reading of imaginative literature, often carried out in the watches of the night.

Education of a more conventional type was received by Chekhov at the gymnasium (grammar school) at Taganrog where Greek and Latin formed a large part of the curriculum. This was a most respectable form of education by the standards of the day, and Chekhov, though no outstanding pupil, was able to proceed to the University of Moscow. There he qualified as a doctor and unofficially as a writer by stories and sketches published during his student years.

Gorky received little formal education, being taught to read by the cook on a Volga steamer for whom he worked as pantry-boy. Of this skill, once acquired, he made excellent use, besides receiving a rough but thorough education in the 'university of life'. He ironically gave the title *My Universities* to the section of his autobiography devoted to what would have been his student years if he had succeeded, as he had hoped, in gaining admission to the University of Kazan.

UNIVERSITIES   The first Russian university, which also had the largest nineteenth-century student body, was that of Moscow, founded in 1755 (4,407 students in 1899). Herzen, who studied there in 1829-33, says that Moscow University had become more and more the focal point of Russian education, since it had all the necessary conditions for development: 'historical importance, geographical position and the absence of the Tsar' (*My Past and Thoughts*, ch. vi).

The University of Derpt, in what is now Estonia, had an especially complex evolution reflecting several centuries of eastern European history. Originally a Swedish foundation in 1632, it was closed in 1710 and reopened by Alexander I in 1802, the language of instruction being German from then until 1895, when it became Russian, the name Derpt having been officially changed back to the town's original Russian name, Yuryev, as part of the drive to russify the periphery of the Empire. To add to these complexities the German name for Derpt is Dorpat and the town is now called Tartu.

The year 1804 saw the foundation of Kazan and Kharkov Universities. In 1819 St Petersburg University was founded, followed by those of Kiev (1833), Odessa (1864), Warsaw (1869) and Tomsk (1888). A step in the opposite direction was the closing of the University of Vilna in 1832. With minor variations each university had four faculties: history and philology; physics and mathematics; law; medicine. St Petersburg had, in addition, a faculty of oriental languages (transferred from Kazan), but no medical faculty, the deficiency being supplied by the St Petersburg Military Medical Academy. Derpt had a fifth faculty, of Lutheran theology. For the higher education of the Orthodox clergy there were four clerical academies (*dukhovnyye akademii*) independent of the universities: those of Kiev, Moscow, St Petersburg and Kazan.

Women were not admitted as university students, but were sporadically provided with a form of university education by 'higher women's courses' started in Moscow in 1869, and also established in St Petersburg, Kazan and Kiev in the 1870s. A Women's Medical Institute was established in St Petersburg. In common with other liberal features of the educational system, facilities for women's education were severely curtailed under Alexander III. University autonomy also suffered during the recurring periods of political oppression. In the freest periods the highest official of each university (the rector), the deans of the faculties and the professors were elected within the universities themselves. But during periods of reaction these officials were directly appointed and dismissed by the ministry of education, or at least such appointments had to be officially ratified. In the early years of the nineteenth century the universities had even exercised control over the secondary and primary schools in their areas, but this function was later removed from them.

After the Crimean War, and increasingly during the rest of the period under review, Russian universities became centres of political unrest. This was the age of student demonstrations, riots and strikes, supported by the more liberal university teachers, who risked dismissal by such displays of sympathy. Peasant disturbances at the time of emancipation and the Khodynka disaster of 1896 (see p. 71) were among occasions evoking student protests. Worse riots followed in St Petersburg University in 1899, provoked by an official warning that unruliness would not be tolerated during the University's annual celebration on 8th February. A student demonstration was dispersed by mounted police with whips, after which a general strike of students was declared and carried out in many other universities too. Student demonstrators were liable to harsh treatment, being sent down from the universities and drafted into the army as privates – it was comparatively easy for the authorities to do this, since the deferment or curtailment of military service, to which students were entitled, conveniently lapsed when they were expelled. But these reprisals only inflamed the situation, and in 1901 a former student carried academic protest to its ultimate limit by assassinating the minister of education, N.P. Bogolepov.

Student unrest was due to political dissatisfaction aggravated by specific grievances, such as the disciplinary powers exercised by university inspectors and a virtual ban on independent corporate activities. Many students were poor, as is not unknown in other countries, and they often lived in squalor, as does the student Raskolnikov in Dostoyevsky's *Crime and Punishment*. Even Raskolnikov was better housed than many of his fellow-students, however, for at least he did not share his miserable St Petersburg garret with anyone else.

Another of literature's well-known undergraduates is Peter Trofimov, the 'eternal student' of Chekhov's *Cherry Orchard*. There are references in the dialogue to his 'already having been sent down from the university twice', and 'having been landed in some pretty queer places', from which it is clear that Soviet commentators are not indulging in special pleading when they claim that Trofimov's creator conceived him as a budding revolutionary. To portray him as such was impossible under censorship conditions of the time, as Chekhov implied in a letter to his wife of 19 October 1903: 'You see, Trofimov is in exile off and on, and gets chucked out of the university every so often, and how is one to depict that sort of thing?'

EDUCATIONAL POLICY AND ORGANISATION   What of educational policy? The relatively liberal phase of Alexander II's reign was preceded and followed by periods of intolerance and repression under Nicholas I and Alexander III. There were some relaxations in the first part of Nicholas II's reign.

Even Alexander II's reign had been educationally liberal only during its first decade. From 1866 to 1880 his minister of education was the extreme reactionary Count D.A. Tolstoy, whose pedagogic views had little in common with those of his more famous namesake the novelist. D.A. Tolstoy's tenure of office saw a large increase in the number of schools and of the pupils attending them, but he closely controlled appointments and syllabuses, particularly those of the gymnasiums (grammar-schools). A feature of his policy was the emphasis laid on the study of Greek and Latin as a means of curbing political unrest. It was believed that concentration on these classical languages, especially on their syntax, would discourage revolutionary sentiments. This proved a vain hope, since the schools in fact became centres of political disaffection – as did, to a far greater extent, the universities which many gymnasium pupils went on to attend.

Chekhov, the only nineteenth-century Russian writer of the front rank to complete a full course at a grammar school, failed to become a political firebrand, but was left with a distaste for Greek and Latin which seems to have haunted him for life. Having received the most intensive classical education among leading Russian writers, he came to write exceptionally disciplined and elegant Russian prose, though how much credit for this can be given to the model of Cicero and Demosthenes is not clear. Using these techniques, Chekhov superbly portrays, in his story *A Hard Case* (1898), a pedantic grammar-school teacher of Greek whose only pleasures are meddling in his colleagues' private lives and rolling the word *anthropos* round his tongue.

In periods of political reaction educational policy-makers aimed to exclude pupils of humble social origin from the gymnasiums and universities. Increases in school and university fees and insistence on irksome formalities were used from time to time to discourage lower-class children from claiming places in these establishments, which should be the monopoly of the gentry, according to opponents of social change. An official circular issued in 1887 proclaimed the need to keep out of the grammar schools the children of coachmen, footmen, cooks, laundresses, small shopkeepers and similar undesirables. This instruction was issued nearly ten years after Chekhov had received his leaving certificate from the Taganrog Gymnasium – otherwise he, the son of a struggling shopkeeper, might have been compelled to seek his schooling elsewhere.

For administrative purposes the Empire was divided into educational areas (*uchebnyye okruga*), of which there were twelve at the end of the nineteenth century. High officials entitled curators (*popechiteli*) were responsible within a given area for all educational institutions coming under the ministry, including universities, gymnasiums and primary schools. The general pattern was for each area to be centred on a single university, the curator's office being in the university city of his area.

SECONDARY SCHOOLS Despite attempts to use dead languages as a political narcotic, the gymnasiums yet provided the best schooling widely available. They were first developed on a significant scale under Alexander I, when the initial aim was to equip every provincial capital with its gymnasium. By the end of the century this modest plan had been over-fulfilled, and there were nearly two hundred gymnasiums in all. The course was virtually uniform throughout Russia. Unsatisfactory pupils were kept down to do a second year in the same form – as happened to Chekhov in both the third and fifth forms owing to his inadequate performance in the annual examinations. There were pro-gymnasiums – similar institutions, offering the first four years of the gymnasium course. There were also modern schools (*realnyye uchilishcha*), which emphasised mathematics, science and modern languages, and gave entry to technical colleges, whereas the gymnasiums qualified their graduates to enter the universities and civil service. The above were all boys' schools, but girls too had their gymnasiums, being better served with secondary school education than they were at either university or primary level. Girls' gymnasiums offered a seven-year course with an extra year for those who wished to qualify as schoolmistresses. They also imposed less Latin and Greek on their pupils.

The church maintained its own secondary schools – the seminaries mentioned above (p. 105). Their programme followed similar lines to that of the gymnasiums, but also included theological material designed to fit pupils to serve the Orthodox Church. There were fifty-five seminaries in 1900 with some 18,000 pupils. The church also maintained diocesan girls' secondary schools, mainly for daughters of the clergy. They were designed to fit girls to become priests' wives and were not academically ambitious. In 1900 there were over sixty of them with about 15,000 pupils.

PRIMARY SCHOOLS The primary schools maintained by the church (see p. 104–5) offered a four-year course designed for, but not exclusive to, children of the clergy. They must not be confused with the much more numerous parish (*tserkovno-prikhodskiye*) schools, which were administered by the church for the population at large, forming a sizeable part of the Empire's primary school system.

Schools of literacy (*shkoly gramoty*) on a lower level still, also came under the Holy Synod, which was administering nearly thirty-five thousand primary schools of all types, with well over a million pupils, at the end of the nineteenth century. In the same year the over-all tally of primary schools throughout the Empire was nearly eighty thousand, with a total of nearly four million pupils. There was only one authority with wider control over primary education than that exercised by the Synod – the ministry of education itself, responsible in 1896 for some two-fifths of the Empire's primary schools with nearly two-thirds of the pupils. At the same time the ministry of war was responsible for over ten thousand primary schools with some three hundred thousand pupils (Kovalevsky, p. 476 ff).

Schools were set up by village communes, by town councils and also by the zemstvos, the zemstvo schools being of particular importance by the end of the nineteenth century. Many schools were founded by private individuals, including writers, and that established at Yasnaya Polyana by Tolstoy in 1859 became especially famous. A noted theorist of education, as of almost everything else in human life, Tolstoy was a devoted teacher of peasant children and produced a fairly successful reading primer, his *ABC Book*, in 1872. Chekhov too founded schools for the peasants during his residence in the village of Melikhovo, south of Moscow, and his story *My Life* illustrates the embarrassments and difficulties which such philanthropy might provoke.

OTHER SCHOOLS Besides the institutions mentioned above, Russia also possessed a variety of boarding-schools, including the quaintly named 'pensions for genteel spinsters'. There were Sunday schools designed to teach, not religious knowledge but reading and writing, and officially suspected as centres of revolutionary agitation. And there were increasing numbers of technical and vocational colleges, including the Moscow Higher Technical School. It also became a common practice for factories to provide schools for the children of employees.

Even by the end of our period this rapidly growing system was on too small a scale for the gigantic Empire. With her large proportion of illiterates, Russia was still far from achieving universal primary education by 1904. And that of girls was particularly neglected. In 1896 less than a quarter of the over-all number of primary school pupils were girls. Hence, perhaps, a favourite proverb of the (male) Russian peasant: 'A woman is long on hair and short on brain.'

17 Press and censorship

IMPORTANCE OF THE PRESS Since most major works of Russian literature first appeared in periodical publication, the literary situation cannot be fully understood without some knowledge of the press and of the workings of censorship. This is also necessary for a general understanding of Russian intellectual life, and of the political conflicts which smouldered and flared throughout the period. Though so many types of publication were subject to censorship, the press provided the most important – at times the only – arena for public debate and for the struggle between the forces of imperial 'law' and liberal or revolutionary 'disorder'.

PERIODICALS The most important vehicles for new literary works were 'thick journals': bulky reviews, mainly monthlies. Besides printing original Russian literature, these published literary criticism and foreign literature in translation, together with philosophical and historical material. Social and political topics – the main concern to many readers and editors – were also extensively ventilated, but it was often necessary to treat them obliquely, circumspectly and allusively.

In the first half of the century the monthly reviews were more influential than the daily or weekly press. This was partly due to the difficulty, at a time of harsher censorship, of reporting and commenting on day-to-day political events, which hampered newspapers and weeklies more than monthlies. It was also due to poor communications. In rural districts the post was not delivered to individual houses, but had to be collected, often from a considerable distance. It might arrive only once a week, and might be delayed by blizzard, flood or cholera quarantine. The monthlies could afford a more leisurely view of Russian and world affairs than was possible for their flimsier competitors, and therefore enjoyed an advantage.

Through them intellectually alert Russian country squires, of whom there were not a few, could keep abreast of cultural trends.

By the 1880s about a dozen such reviews were in being, with circulations rising to nine or ten thousand each. It was possible to finance a journal on a subscription list of only a few thousand, and these organs had influence out of all proportion to their readership, partly because the proportion of intellectuals in the population was so small. Moreover, the monthlies enjoyed greater freedom of speech than was conceded to any other medium except books – more leniently censored, but less immediate in impact.

After Alexander II had opened the press to relatively free political discussion a new social phenomenon appeared – the newspaper campaign. War news enhanced the importance of the daily newspaper during the Crimean War (1853–6), and patriotic press campaigns were fought against the Poles during the Polish revolt of 1863, and against the Turks before and during the Russo-Turkish War of 1877–8.

Even in the grim days of Nicholas I a periodical could have a political slant. The widely despised *Northern Bee* (St Petersburg, 1825–64), edited by F. Bulgarin, was for a time the only daily newspaper entitled to receive political information, and was almost an organ of the government since it was largely controlled by the Third Section of the imperial chancery. Other periodicals kept up some degree of political opposition, and in the middle years of the century the best known of these was *The Contemporary*.

'THE CONTEMPORARY' AND 'NOTES OF THE FATHERLAND'   *The Contemporary* had been founded by Pushkin, but its period of greatest influence began in 1846, when it was bought by Nekrasov. For a short time before his death Belinsky was the journal's chief literary critic. Later critics and social theorists included Dobrolyubov and Chernyshevsky. *The Contemporary* published most of Turgenev's *Sportsman's Sketches* from 1847 onwards, and his first two novels, *Rudin* and *A Nest of Gentlefolk*. It also first published Tolstoy's *Childhood, Boyhood* and *Youth*. *The Contemporary* was closed in 1866 in the wave of restrictions following the attempt on the Tsar's life in that year. Nekrasov now went over to *Notes of the Fatherland* (St Petersburg, 1839–84), which had published Belinsky's early critical works, Goncharov's *Oblomov* and two early novels of Dostoyevsky, *The Double* and *The Village of Stepanchikovo* (1859). In

1875 Dostoyevsky returned to *Notes of the Fatherland* with his long and comparatively disappointing novel *A Raw Youth*.

M.N. KATKOV AND 'THE RUSSIAN HERALD' As the last-mentioned episode suggests, Nekrasov could not compete with the conservative publisher and journalist M.N. Katkov in attracting Russia's foremost novelists. It was Katkov's review *The Russian Herald* (Moscow, 1856–87; Moscow and St Petersburg, 1887–1906) which first published all four of Dostoyevsky's greatest novels: *Crime and Punishment*, *The Idiot*, *Devils* and *The Brothers Karamazov*. Katkov also brought out three of Turgenev's four last novels (*On the Eve*, *Fathers and Children* and *Smoke*) as well as *War and Peace* (in part) and *Anna Karenin* (Parts One to Seven). Thus nine of the ten most significant works of Russian fiction published between 1860 and 1880 all first appeared in this one review. The exception was Turgenev's *Virgin Soil*, published in the *European Herald* (St Petersburg, 1866–1918).

Katkov has not always had credit for these *coups*, perhaps through disapproval of his political views. In Mirsky's *History of Russian Literature*, for example, *The Russian Herald* does not even rate a mention, though there is much information on *The Contemporary* and *Notes of the Fatherland*. Katkov showed great tact in nursing the highly emotional and financially helpless Dostoyevsky, and was a notable literary impresario. But Katkov could also behave autocratically when he disapproved of an author's material. He refused to print Part Eight of Tolstoy's *Anna Karenin* because he deplored Tolstoy's scathing attitude to the Russian quarrel with Turkey, and he it was who banned the notorious chapter in Dostoyevsky's *Devils* – never subsequently restored by the author – where Stavrogin confesses to the rape of a little girl.

OTHER PUBLICATIONS After Katkov's death in 1887 there were no major novels to scoop, and new names appear among the journals which printed leading literary works. Chekhov's career shows a writer working his way up from the bottom of the ladder. He began in a trivial comic weekly, *The Dragonfly* (St Petersburg, 1857–1908) and then published in other minor organs such as *Alarm Clock* (Moscow, 1873–1917) and the weekly *Splinters* (St Petersburg, 1881–1916) before graduating upwards by way of two newspapers, the *St Petersburg Gazette* and the influential conservative *New Time*

(St Petersburg, 1868–1917). Then came his début in the 'thick journals' when the monthly *Northern Herald* (St Petersburg, 1885–98) published his long story *Steppe* in 1888, after which Chekhov remained a 'thick journal' man for life. He published in several, but it was the liberal monthly *The Russian Idea* (Moscow, 1880–1918) which produced the bulk of his longer and better-known stories, including *Ward No 6* (1892), *An Anonymous Story*, *Three Years*, *Peasants* and *The Lady with the Dog* (1899). Chekhov happily published in all shades of the press from the conservative *New Time*, an unfashionable platform for an author who wished to impress the Russian intelligentsia, to the Marxist *Life* (St Petersburg, 1897–1901); though he gradually moved leftwards in his choice of vehicle. *Life* incidentally published Gorky's two earliest novels, *Foma Gordeyev* and *Three of Them* (1900–1). The latter was not printed in full in *Life*, but was cut off in mid-career when the review was banned in June 1901.

THE CENSOR'S TASK AND PROBLEMS   Imperial Russian thought-control was mainly negative. The authorities sought to suppress subversive notions – atheistic, revolutionary and so on – but were less concerned to inculcate improving ideas. They were more eager to keep unwanted matter out than to ram official ideology down readers' throats. It was a censorship of morals, as well as of politics and religion. Even such a modest writer as Chekhov was often forced to suppress details about the sexual relations between his characters, and also to tone down domestic quarrels, so that his stories might be suitable for 'family reading'.

In general Russian nineteenth-century censorship was relatively insensitive in the realm of ideas, being more concerned with matters of fact and with personalities. Greatly varying in severity, always unpredictable, it was an abiding cause of apprehension, frustration and embarrassment even to those writers, editors and publishers who were least engaged in crusading against church and state.

Absurd examples of censors' interference are often quoted, such as the ban on the phrases 'forces of nature' and 'free currents of air', and the insistence (presumably to deter would-be Tsaricides) that Roman emperors always 'perished', and were never 'killed'. Musical scores were suspected of cloaking sinister cyphered messages, and one censor even objected to a poet calling a woman's smile 'celestial' because such praise might be considered blasphemous (Rozenberg, p. 40). Nor did the very censors avoid acute harassment. At one time a special committee was set up to censor censors. A censor could be punished for *lack of vigilance*, a fundamental Russian concept throughout the ages, and could be arrested and confined to a military guardhouse like a mere author. Censors often objected to harmless material simply in order to show that they were alert. They could be dismissed or suspended, as happened to the censor who passed Chaadayev's *Philosophical Letter* for publication in the Moscow *Telescope* in 1834. The censor who passed Turgenev's *Sportsman's Sketches* was also dismissed. But though censoring was no sinecure, some writers were prepared to undertake it and police their own colleagues. The best known was Goncharov, whom one hardly sees as the watchdog of imperial authority or indeed of anything else. The poet Tyutchev and the critic and thinker Konstantin Leontyev, both extreme conservatives, also worked as censors.

PENALTIES Disciplinary measures included warnings, reprimands, rebukes, fines, confiscations of offending periodicals, exile, police surveillance and – a typical feature of Nicholas I's reign – detention in the guardhouse of some local garrison unit. Isolated words and phrases might be cut or whole paragraphs, items and editions banned. Publications were often closed down. For example, in 1834 the fortnightly *Moscow Telegraph* (Moscow, from 1825) was banned for printing an unfavourable review of a patriotic play, *The Hand of the Almighty Saved the Fatherland*, by N.V. Kukolnik. In 1836 the fortnightly, later weekly, *Telescope* (Moscow, from 1831) was banned for printing the first of Chaadayev's *Philosophical Letters*, in which Russian civilisation was denounced. In 1866, as noted above, Nekrasov's *Contemporary* was closed down, and *Notes of the Fatherland*, to which Nekrasov went over in 1868, was in turn closed down in 1884. The Marxist journal *Life*, which published much of Gorky's early work, was banned in 1901, as noted above (p. 160). Left-wing publications were not the only victims. Conservative and slavophile organs also suffered interference, as did those with no definite political slant. In 1863 Dostoyevsky's review *Time* (started in 1861) was banned because of an article, on the Polish rebellion, wrongly interpreted by officials as an attack on government policy. Dostoyevsky then founded a new review, *The Epoch*,

but was forced to abandon it in 1865 because he had lost his readership, and he now faced financial ruin. Reviews could also be crippled
by less drastic means – for instance, by the imposition of a ban on
the publication of advertisements, often a main source of revenue.

PRE-REFORM CENSORSHIP   Russian censorship was a child of the
nineteenth century, though interference, often by the church, had
been common before. Vague censorship regulations were brought
in under Catherine the Great, in whose reign two leading writers,
Radishchev (in 1790) and Novikov (in 1792) were imprisoned and
exiled. The former was even sentenced to death, commuted to ten
years' Siberian exile, for writing his *Journey from St Petersburg to
Moscow*, a travelogue which assails the institutions of serfdom and
autocracy. But it was not until 1804, early in the reign of Alexander
I, that the first comprehensive censorship statute was enacted.
Under the new Tsar censorship policy was at first tolerant, but grew
harsher and became especially so under Nicholas I. It was at its most
severe from 1848 to 1855, the age of 'terror by censorship', as it
came to be called.

Yet it was in these very terror-dominated years that the flourishing realist movement arose – at the time when, according to the contemporary diarist A.V. Nikitenko, the number of officials engaged
in censorship exceeded the total number of volumes published in
a year (Rozenberg, p. 54). Among the bodies censoring or controlling literature at various times between 1804 and 1855 were: the
ministry of education, the military authorities, the church, the universities, the Second and Third Sections of the imperial chancery,
the ministry of transport, the ministry of police, the railway authorities, the commission supervising the building of St Isaac's Cathedral
in St Petersburg and even the administration of state horse-
breeding.

PUSHKIN AND THE CENSORSHIP   The censorship's most famous
martyr was Pushkin. After his release in 1826 from exile to his family
estate at Mikhaylovskoye, Nicholas I said that he would act as Pushkin's personal censor. Pushkin was delighted, believing that he
could go ahead and publish his newly completed verse drama, *Boris
Godunov*, but was reprimanded by the Chief of Gendarmes, Count
Benckendorff, merely for reading the unpublished play aloud in
Moscow literary circles without first submitting it to the Tsar. It

then turned out that the special relationship between Pushkin and the Tsar was simply an extra encumbrance since the poet was to remain subject to the regular censorship as well.

Pushkin even received technical literary advice from the most august quarter when the Tsar, through Benckendorff, offered the following comment on *Boris Godunov*: 'I consider that Mr Pushkin's aim would be fulfilled if, along with *necessary expurgation*, he would change his drama to a historical tale or novel, similar to Walter Scott's' (letter of 14 December 1826). Pushkin replied frigidly: 'I have received with profound gratitude Your Excellency's letter informing me of His Majesty's most gracious comment on my dramatic poem. I agree that it resembles a historical novel more than a tragedy, as the Sovereign Emperor has deigned to observe. I am sorry that it is beyond my power to recast what I have once written' (letter of 3 January 1827). Pushkin's play was ready for the press in 1826, but it was not until 1831, and then as a special favour so that he could meet expenses connected with his marriage, that he was permitted to publish.

Among many works denied publication through censorship, or mutilated by censorship before they did appear, were two political poems of Pushkin's youth: *Freedom* (written 1817; first published in Russian in London in 1856; first published in Russia in 1906) and *The Village* (written 1819; first published in truncated form in Russia in 1826; first published in full in Russian in London in 1856; first published in full in Russia in 1870). Pushkin's long blasphemous poem *Gavriiliada* was written in 1821, but first published in London in 1861.

OTHER VICTIMS Other works to suffer included Griboyedov's *Woe from Wit* and Lermontov's poems *The Demon* and *Death of a Poet*. Pisemsky's novel *Boyarshchina* (written in 1845, published in 1858) and Chekhov's short play *On the High Road* (submitted for censorship in 1885 and published posthumously) were both banned as too gloomy. From Tolstoy's novel *Resurrection* a scene satirising the Orthodox church service was cut, and some five hundred alterations in all were imposed by the censorship; not until 1936 did a full version of the novel eventually appear. Dostoyevsky's most important short work, *Memoirs from Underground* (1864) was ruined, he said, by 'those swine of censors' who 'banned the section where I deduced the need for a belief in Christ' (letter of 26 March

1864). The missing passage was not restored by the author and has been lost. Then there was also self-censorship, such as is inevitably practised in an atmosphere of excessive control over literature. Chekhov, for instance, wrote that his story *My Life* (1896) was 'bound to make a mutilated impression [despite the fact that cuts imposed by the censorship had later been restored when the story appeared in book form] as when I wrote it I could not forget for one moment that I was writing for a magazine subject to censorship' (Vinogradov, ed., *Chekhov: Literaturnoye nasledstvo*, p. 213).

THE REFORMED CENSORSHIP   From 1804 to 1865 censorship was basically preventive in the sense that all material must be submitted for approval to one or more authorities before publication. But it was also punitive – that is, a censor's prior approval was no guarantee that objections would not be raised at a later stage. With the accession of Alexander II in 1855 censorship was applied more liberally in the atmosphere of impending reform, and in 1865 new regulations were introduced. Termed 'temporary', they yet remained in force for forty years.

The main effect was to whittle down preventive censorship. All original books of ten or more printed pages, and all translated works of twenty or more printed pages, could now be printed without being submitted for prior approval. So too could publications of learned societies, and editions or translations of ancient Greek and Latin literature, for even these had been liable to be mutilated or 'corrected' under Nicholas I.

Under the new regulations periodicals were more strictly censored than books – for which reason Chekhov sometimes reconciled himself to cuts imposed on work published in the periodical press, knowing that he could later restore his text when he came to publish it in a book. Periodicals too were permitted greater latitude under the new regulations. Editors might now choose between preventive and punitive control, and the latter, though it might sound more forbidding, was in practice less restrictive. But this provision applied only to the St Petersburg and Moscow press, preventive censorship remaining mandatory in the provinces – a provision which reinforced the intellectual dominance of the two capitals.

Censorship was mainly exercised by the ministry of the interior after 1865, but church censorship continued to function and there was a special and irksome theatrical censorship. Though censors had become less troublesome, publications still suffered extensive interference, which naturally fluctuated according to changes in the political climate. Under Alexander III, as might be expected, conditions were severe. Censorship remained an obstacle to the free development of Russian literature, unless an irritating and clumsy yet not quite crushing system of official control may actually be a stimulus.

EVASIVE TACTICS Elaborate official regulations often provoke elaborate devices for evading them. Russian censorship was no exception, and despite all obstacles writers still found means of communicating. One technique was indirect allusion in 'Aesopic' language, a term invented by the satirist Saltykov-Shchedrin. The method did not necessarily involve the use of fables, as the name Aesop implies, for any suitable indirect statement would do. Well able to take a hint, the intellectually hungry Russian reader was an expert at reading between the lines.

Censorship was also evaded by the clandestine circulation of manuscripts. Documents circulating in this way included Griboyedov's play *Woe from Wit*, passed from hand to hand for five years before it was performed or published. Even after publication it continued to be passed round because the first published version contained only the woe, according to one contemporary. The wit had all been censored out (Monas, p. 184). Lermontov's *Death of a Poet* was also handed round in this way. So too were many of Pushkin's poems including his *Village*, *Freedom* and *Gavriiliada*, and other celebrated documents, including Chaadayev's *Philosophical Letter*, much of Tolstoy's theoretical work and Belinsky's open letter to Gogol, which became a manifesto of the radical opposition. Handling such material was potentially dangerous, as Dostoyevsky found when sentenced to death for reading out Belinsky's letter, among other crimes against the state.

Evasion also took many other forms. There was the habit of denouncing political articles in the foreign press, with lavish quotation designed to give them publicity in the only way possible – a subterfuge which, like many another evasive technique practised under the Tsars, has survived into modern times. Russian periodicals were sometimes published abroad to be smuggled into Russia. The first important instance was *The Bell*, published in London by Herzen and Ogaryov from 1857 to 1865, then in Geneva for two years. The same editors also brought out an annual, *The Pole Star*, in London from 1855 to 1862.

FOREIGN MATTER   The fate of foreign works on Russian soil was erratic. One surprising import was Karl Marx's *Capital*, which no censor detected as a Trojan horse. The first volume appeared in Russia in Russian translation in 1872 before it had been translated into any other language. But works by Herbert Spencer and Darwin, and even by Heine and Flaubert, were banned or mutilated.

Foreign books and periodicals imported into the Empire in their original languages were censored by a special organ, the 'foreign censorship'. This had branches in Moscow and St Petersburg where foreign material was scrutinised for passages offensive to the Russian government, and these were then laboriously deleted. According to a British observer of these proceedings: 'With a preparation of gutta-percha and powdered glass he [the Moscow censor of foreign printed matter] will cleanse and purify *The Times* of a paragraph, or *Punch* of a joke, in so neat a manner that not a vestige of printer's ink shall remain' (Edwards, p. 32).

18 The opposition

VARIETIES OF DISAFFECTION   In the present chapter elements of
disintegration and political opposition in imperial Russian society
will be considered. They present a confusing picture, since the
Empire's internal opponents had no common platform, but
differed from each other in numerous ways – most significantly in
the degree of their addiction to violence. At one end of the scale
were advocates of liberal reform, though even the seemingly mild
designation 'liberal' had a special resonance – in nineteenth-century
Russia the phrase 'a dangerous liberal' by no means seemed a con-
tradiction in terms, as it now might. At the other extreme were dedicated political assassins, heroes to some and monsters to others.
They included the five young people who were clumsily executed
by a drunken hangman in the Semyonovsky Square in St Petersburg
after slaughtering Alexander II with home-made bombs.

Though antagonism to the autocracy came chiefly from the left
wing, there was also some opposition from diehard conservatives
hostile to Alexander II's reforms. Deploring the emancipation
of their serfs and the new restrictions on corporal punishment,
they were sometimes called 'planters' by radical journalists accustomed to compare serfdom in Russia with slavery in the United
States. As will be remembered, the same decade saw the end of
both.

Not all landowning gentlemen were 'planters'. For example, in
1862 the gentry of Tver sent a formal petition to Alexander II asking
for political rights to be granted to the entire people (they were wil-
ling to renounce their own privileged position), and thirteen of
them, who later put their names to a more outspoken document
on the same lines, were imprisoned for a time. These were actions
in favour of liberal reform by members of the gentry acting cor-
porately. Individual gentlemen were also prominent as theorists and

practitioners of reform and revolution throughout the century, being well to the fore as both oppressors and oppressed.

For left-wing Russian oppositionists many different terms have been used: Liberals, Progressives, Radicals, Socialists, Populists, Nihilists, Anarchists, Revolutionaries, Marxists, Communists and Terrorists. Some of these labels overlap with and fuse into each other, being neither interchangeable nor mutually exclusive. Specific illegal political parties and conspiratorial groups (such as Land and Freedom and the Socialist Revolutionary Party) must also be taken into account, besides which such important concepts as those of the intelligentsia and slavophilism have to be considered as well.

WESTERNISTS AND SLAVOPHILES   Two main currents – those of westernism and slavophilism – are often distinguished in Russian social and political thinking. The term 'westernist' is applied to those who, however widely they might differ on other matters, were united in believing that Russia was essentially European and that she should learn from and imitate western Europe. Belinsky held westernist views, as also did the other radical thinkers Cherny-shevsky, Dobrolyubov and Pisarev. Another westernist was Bakunin, the founder of modern political anarchism, who originally formed a model for the westernist Turgenev's Rudin. After protests by sympathisers of Bakunin, Turgenev changed his portrait to the point where Chernyshevsky conceded that it was no longer even a recognisable caricature of Bakunin (Turgenev, *Sobraniye sochineny*, ii, pp. 313–14), and it is true that Rudin in his final form pales beside the ebullient Bakunin. Westernists also included T.N. Granovsky, a liberal professor of history at Moscow University who served as the prototype for Stephen Verkhovensky in the anti-wes-ternist Dostoyevsky's *Devils*. Stephen, father of the nihilist villain Peter Verkhovensky, is condemned by Dostoyevsky, who tended to lump liberals and revolutionaries together. Each, in his view, suffered from the same disease – what matter, then, if one had it in milder form, when both were equally dangerous sources of infec-tion? Dostoyevsky thus dissented from the common practice of con-trasting the 'fathers' of the 1840s with the 'sons' of the 1860s, regard-ing the generations as equally heretical.

Though the trends represented by westernism and slavophilism may be traced in earlier Russian history, it was not until the 1840s that they split into two sharply opposed camps engaged in extensive controversy with each other. Their clashes are portrayed in Turgenev's novel *Smoke*.

Since the slavophiles supported the principle of autocracy, there is a tendency to think of them as enthusiasts for the imperial system. This view was not, however, shared by Nicholas I's censors and police officials. Though the slavophiles were by no means revolutionaries, the very fact that they included notable original thinkers made them an object of official mistrust – especially under Nicholas I, when the very act of expressing an opinion, even in support of the government, aroused the authorities' suspicions. The slavophiles advocated the emancipation of the serfs and differed from the westernists in their assessment of Peter the Great, the most active of all Russian westernists, whose influence on the country's development they deplored. They attached importance to the village commune as a traditional Slav institution, to the Orthodox Church, to the collection of folk-lore material – in fact to everything covered by the charismatic and untranslatable word *narodny* (popular, national, folksy, essentially Russian) from which *narodnik* ('populist') derives. Gogol and Dostoyevsky may be regarded as slavophiles, and another important writer associated with the movement was S.T. Aksakov, whose sons Konstantin and Ivan became important theorists of the movement. The slavophiles lost impetus in the 1860s.

THE FORTIES AND SIXTIES   The 1840s had been an age of intellectual ferment more philosophical in character than were the concerns of many political oppositionists from the 1860s onwards. It was the interpretation of German and French philosophers and social thinkers, rather than the manufacture of bombs, which interested the men of the forties. They also attached greater importance to aesthetic and cultural values than did the later 'nihilist' movement, which tended to judge art solely from the point of view of utility – witness the nihilist cliché to the effect that a good pair of boots was more valuable than the entire works of Pushkin. There is thus a marked contrast between oppositionists of the two decades – the older generation being polite, philosophical, romantic and emotional (see Herzen's long accounts of his love affairs and sentimental friendships), while the younger men were brusque, 'realistic', down-to-earth and more concerned with revolutionary action. The first was the age of circles and discussion groups, the second that

of conspiracies. This was also a contrast between patrician and plebeian, between talk and action, and in literature between Turgenev's *Fathers and Children* in his novel with that title.

THE INTELLIGENTSIA The term intelligentsia originated in
Russia, where (by contrast with its use in the present-day Soviet
Union and as applied to other countries) it generally referred only
to 'that part of educated society which held radical left-wing views'
(Utechin, *Dictionary*, p. 235). Consequently a leading intellectual
such as Dostoyevsky cannot properly be called a member of the Russian intelligentsia, since he was a militant conservative, at least in
later life. He would not himself have wished to be regarded as an
intelligent (the Russian word for a member of the intelligentsia) –
and in fact he lost few opportunities to denounce the intelligentsia.
His view is not on the whole shared by students of the period, who
have been inclined to praise *intelligenty* for their courage and high-
mindedness, but he was not alone among the better-known Russian
writers in taking so jaundiced a view.

Chekhov too had moods of impatience with the Russian intelligentsia, which he once described as 'hypocritical, false, hysterical,
uneducated and lazy' (letter of 22 February 1899). But his views
on the subject were not consistent – it would, indeed, be absurd to
look for consistency in his casual asides. On balance he shows himself an advocate of the intelligentsia, while distrusting those representatives of it who were most extreme in their political views.
Whether through personal distaste or censorship conditions, he is
rarely found portraying a significant type of his age – the Russian
revolutionary – though he did so in somewhat muted form in his
Anonymous Story. He was appalled by the extreme intolerance of
Russian political oppositionists. 'Under the flag of science, art and
persecuted freedom of thought', he once claimed, Russia would one
day be ruled by 'toads and crocodiles the like of which were unknown even in Spain at the time of the Inquisition' (letter of 27
August 1888).

REVOLUTIONARIES AND NIHILISTS Through the history of Russian nineteenth- and twentieth-century revolutionaries two themes
run in counterpoint. First there is 'action' – much of it bizarre and
far-fetched in the extreme. It included burrowing tunnels under
roads and railways over which the Tsar might be expected to pass;

the shooting, stabbing and bombing of police officials, ministers, governor-generals and grand dukes; daring robberies ('expropriations') conducted to provide revolutionary funds; secret printing presses; pamphlets calling on the peasantry to massacre the landlords; penetration of revolutionary cells by police spies and counterpenetration of the police by revolutionary spies. Hysteria, courage, treachery, obstinacy, recklessness, self-sacrifice – all are amply illustrated in the history of Russian revolution.

Meanwhile theoretical argument also festered. What was the role of the peasantry to be in the coming revolution? Of the urban proletariat? Must Russia pass through the stage of capitalism like the advanced countries of western Europe? Or could she take her own path and found socialism on such traditional institutions as the village commune and the artels (workers' associations)? Who should be exterminated? The Tsar alone? The imperial family as a whole? All members of the privileged classes? One tenth of the human race? A half? Nine tenths? These and kindred topics were endlessly canvassed, some in plain or disguised form in the pages of the press, others in illegal pamphlets or conspiratorial meetings. Individuals dabbled in ink or dynamite according to temperament, and many were adept with both.

No comprehensive description of the theory or practice of Russian revolution need be attempted in the present study. This is partly because many accounts already exist, and partly because censorship made it impossible for writers to illustrate the revolutionary struggle frankly and openly in imaginative literature, where it does nevertheless play a certain role.

An important fictional study of Russian revolutionaries is that in Dostoyevsky's novel *Devils*. As an enthusiastic supporter of the autocracy, Dostoyevsky was less hampered by censorship than were authors more sympathetic to political opposition. His study is, accordingly, not a balanced picture of the Russian political situation, but a ferociously intemperate denunciation of the Russian revolutionary movement. It was, however, based on some knowledge of the facts. Dostoyevsky's arch-villain, Peter Verkhovensky, is modelled on a grotesque and violent figure from real life, the revolutionary conspirator Sergey Nechayev. Dostoyevsky even used Nechayev's name for his villain in the draft notes which he made for the novel. The main episode of *Devils*, the murder of Shatov, is based on the actual murder of the student Ivanov, organised by

Nechayev on 21 November 1869 because he had challenged Nechayev's authority within the group. The emphasis on deception, including the pretence of controlling a vast and largely imaginary organisation of secret cells, is also taken from Nechayev's biography. Nechayev himself escaped to Switzerland after Ivanov's murder, but was extradited to Russia and confined in the Fortress of St Peter and St Paul in St Petersburg. Here he won over some of his guards, and in early 1881 even managed to correspond from his cell with members of the People's Will group at the time when they were plotting the assassination of Alexander II. Nechayev died in the fortress dungeons in 1883.

Devils describes the moral disintegration of an unnamed provincial town, brought about by the nihilists of whom Peter Verkhovensky is the leader. The concept of nihilism is elusive and the word has no exact or generally accepted meaning – yet describes an important social phenomenon of the mid-nineteenth century, especially of the 1860s. It is one of those unfortunate terms which are both descriptive and abusive. Dostoyevsky himself tended to apply it to all those whose political views were to the left of his own – a high proportion, one is tempted to say, of the human race. He was also fond of the pejorative derivative *nigilyatina* ('nihilist carrion').

It is not to Dostoyevsky, but to another novelist – Turgenev – that the distinction of first popularising the term 'nihilist' belongs. In his *Fathers and Children*, the most important fictional study of nihilism after *Devils*, he attempts a sympathetic portrait of the type. His hero, Bazarov, is however chiefly memorable for his general rudeness or brusqueness, certainly a common nihilist characteristic, rather than for any attractive positive qualities.

The features of a typical nihilist were: being a student; wearing unconventional dress; long hair (for men), short hair (for women); the preaching and practice of free love; devotion to the rights of women; also, on the theoretical side, materialism, utilitarianism, atheism and a belief in science and human welfare. Anyone exhibiting a significant number of the above indicators was liable to be dismissed as a nihilist by non-sympathisers, besides which the word was often used as a vague synonym for 'revolutionary'. As the above description shows, it is by no means accurate to accuse nihilists of believing in nothing (*nihil*). Even if Pisarev, who is considered the main real-life nihilist, did once put forward the much-quoted axiom that 'whatever can be smashed must be smashed', he did at least add: 'Whatever survives a blow has value.' Unlike most of those termed nihilists, Pisarev was prepared to accept this abusive label as applying to those who shared his views, though he preferred the term 'realist'.

Another important Russian novel is a militant defence of those whom non-sympathisers dismissed as nihilists – Chernyshevsky's *What is to be Done?* (1863), written in prison. This became the Bible of politically disaffected young Russians, though its merits as a work of literature are modest. Indeed it now reads as an unintentionally comic work, if one can forget the circumstances in which it was written and the harsh fate suffered by its author, whose life makes a more memorable story than his fiction. A heroic, bespectacled figure of inflexible will and unshakable opposition to the autocracy, he became a martyr to imprisonment and exile. Before being despatched to Siberia he was subjected in St Petersburg to the ludicrous ceremony of public disgrace, called civil execution and sometimes inflicted on revolutionaries as a prelude to imprisonment and exile. In accordance with the prescribed ritual, Chernyshevsky had a sword ceremonially broken over his head, after being conveyed to a 'pillar of shame' on a scaffold especially erected in a public square. One eye-witness claimed that the prisoner spent the time while the sentence was being read spitting 'with sublime nonchalance' (Gernet, ii, p. 279).

POPULISTS Herzen was at one time an all-out westernist, but after emigrating in 1847 found his enthusiasm cooled by exposure to western Europe as it was and not as he had imagined it. He came to agree with the slavophiles on the importance of the Russian village commune, though its value to him was that it seemed to offer Russia the prospect of a short cut to socialism. The link thus established between westernism and slavophilism makes Herzen the originator of Russian populism.

Populism arose in the 1870s, when – as later – it was notable for two contrasting modes of activity. The first was peaceful, the so-called 'movement to the people', which took place in 1873–4 when hundreds of young men and women went to the Russian villages to influence the peasantry and thus solve the basic crux among Russian revolutionary problems: how to make contact with the inarticulate elements among the forces of disintegration, the peasant masses. The attempt failed, leading to the arrest and trial of many who took part – a theme in Turgenev's last novel, *Virgin Soil*. In 1877 the populists formed a secret political party, Land and Freedom. But they could not agree over the crucial issue of violence, and in 1879 they split into two factions, reformist and terrorist. Members of the former adopted the name Black Repartition, and wished to promote agrarian reform through land redistribution. Not believing in political solutions, they were opposed to terrorism as a political weapon. The other faction, which adopted terrorist tactics, was People's Will. Its members included the serf's son Zhelyabov and his mistress Sophia Perovsky, daughter of a high official, and a notable 'drop-out' of the period. They made attempt after attempt on the life of Alexander II, culminating in the successful assassination by the Yekaterininsky Canal on 1 March 1881.

The accession of a tough-minded monarch, Alexander III, and the rigorous measures taken against the revolutionary movement during his reign, led to a slump in populism as expressed in violence. The unsuccessful attempt to assassinate the Tsar in 1887 – by Lenin's elder brother Alexander Ulyanov, among others – was thus out of character with the general tenor of the 1880s, when oppositionists followed a more modest policy, sometimes termed that 'of little deeds'. Their new strategy was to postpone all hope of revolutionary upheaval, and to concentrate on helping and getting to know the peasant, for example by working as a doctor or teacher for one of the zemstvos. The populists operated both illegally and legally. They published openly, their two main journals being *Notes of the Fatherland* and *Russian Wealth* (St Petersburg, 1880–1918). The main influence on these two publications was the leading theoretician of the movement, N.K. Mikhaylovsky. Another important populist leader was P.L. Lavrov, author of the influential *Historical Letters* (1870), and chiefly active as an émigré.

Populist ideas were expressed by not a few novelists of peasant life, including two minor figures, N.N. Zlatovratsky and P.V. Zasodimsky, who followed the tradition of idealising rural Russia. A more balanced view of the village is found in the work of another populist, Ertel, whose long novel *The Gardenins* (1889) is a major work in Russian peasant fiction. Another writer associated with the movement is Gleb Uspensky, who became disillusioned with populism and left some especially sour pictures of peasant conditions in his *Power of the Soil* (1882). Korolenko too was associated with populism, being one of the most important and determined oppositionists among Russian authors, both as a journalist and as an imaginative writer. He evoked sympathy for oppressed national minorities, in his story *Makar's Dream*, and denounced the misdeeds of the imperial police and law-courts. His sketch *A Strange Girl* (1880) contains a description of a young revolutionary.

SOCIALIST REVOLUTIONARIES   Populism rallied towards the end of the century under the reign of a new and relatively weak-willed Tsar, Nicholas II. In 1902 a new underground party, that of the Socialist Revolutionaries, was formed. It was basically, but not exclusively, a peasant-orientated movement, placing its faith, according to populist tradition, in the village commune. One aim of the party was to socialise land and give it to the peasantry, with periodical redistributions as necessary and without compensation to the landowners. But the most spectacular feature of Socialist Revolutionary policy was its revival of the old People's Will tactic of political assassination.

MARXISTS   Disagreeing with the Socialist Revolutionaries over the policy of political assassination, the Russian Marxist movement rejected political terror on the grounds that it did not produce results, and certainly not through sentiment or squeamishness. The main point at issue between Socialist Revolutionaries and Marxists was the peasantry. Marxists regarded it as a backward force, inferior in revolutionary potential to the urban proletariat, and it was their habit to use a formula utterly unacceptable to the Socialist Revolutionaries: 'the idiocy of rural life'.

Marxists also rejected the populist contention that Russia was to follow a special historical evolution of its own. They believed that the country must pass through the phase of capitalism like any ordinary western European state lacking the advantages – which to Marxists were of dubious importance – of Russian corporate institutions. As already stated, Russian was the first foreign language into which Marx's *Capital* was translated. G.V. Plekhanov, the main founder of Russian Marxism, had been a leading theorist in the Land and Freedom movement between 1876 and 1879. When, in the latter year, the movement split into a reformist and terrorist wing, he headed the former, but shortly after emigrating in 1880 broke with populism and became a Marxist, founding a Marxist group abroad, the Liberation of Labour.

From the 1880s illegal Marxist groups were meeting in Russia. The Russian Social Democratic Labour Party, founded secretly in 1898, brought them together and was the lineal forerunner of the present Communist Party of the Soviet Union. Its early history includes the ascendancy acquired by Lenin and the split into the two factions of Bolshevik and Menshevik in 1903. Russian Marxists were to prove most effective on the conspiratorial level, but also pursued their 'legal' activities – for instance, they published the magazine *Life* in which some of Gorky's work appeared.

Gorky became the most celebrated writer to support Bolshevism, but had aroused the authorities' suspicions long before the Social Democratic Party was founded. After being arrested in 1888 for associating with a subversive group, he was under constant police supervision. Other episodes in his career include being expelled from Nizhny Novgorod in 1901, and – in the following year – having his election as an honorary member of the Imperial Academy of Sciences annulled at the personal initiative of Nicholas II. (The episode led Chekhov and Korolenko to resign their own honorary membership of the Academy out of sympathy with Gorky.) In 1905 Gorky increased his revolutionary qualifications by being briefly imprisoned in the Fortress of St Peter and St Paul and by meeting Lenin for the first time.

Dazzled by the terrorist tactics of the Socialist Revolutionaries, the imperial authorities had been slow to discern danger from Russia's Marxists, who at first seemed dull, doctrinaire creatures bogged down in economic abstractions and less apt with dynamite and pistol than the picturesque heirs of People's Will. Only when it was too late did the authorities find that they had to take their Marxists more seriously.

TOLSTOY AND THE OPPOSITION   Though revolutionary activity could not be adequately reflected in contemporary literature, one work containing detailed portraits of revolutionaries is Tolstoy's *Resurrection*. Here Catherine Maslov's companions in prison and exile provide the opportunity for a number of revolutionary studies. For instance, some features in the revolutionary Marya Shchetin are based on a real-life prototype, N.A. Armfeld. In the same novel Nekhlyudov's attempts to intercede for imprisoned revolutionaries include an interview with a certain 'Baron Kriegsmuth', the real-life Baron Von Maydel, Commandant of the Fortress of St Peter and St Paul, which Tolstoy himself visited and where hundreds of revolutionaries were held in the course of the century. The relaxation, amounting almost to abolition, of censorship after the 1905 Revolution, made more outspoken studies of the phenomenon possible in such works as Gorky's *Mother*. Two notable stories by Leonid Andreyev, *The Governor* (1906) and *Seven Who Were Hanged* (1908), are based on the theme of political assassination, but these and similar works take us outside the period of the present study.

If it should be asked which individual among the great Russian writers contributed most to the disintegration of the monarchy and of imperial society, the answer must surely be Tolstoy. He rejected violence and was more a pacifist-anarchist than a revolutionary. But he battered away with persistent eloquence against the traditional allegiances of the Russian Empire, as against the trappings of modern civilisation in general. Should the imperial Russian citizen pay his taxes, defend his country, respect its law-courts and its social structure? Should he even sleep with his wife? To all these questions Tolstoy answered a resounding and impressively reasoned 'no'. His powerful arguments, widely circulated both legally and in clandestine copies, had an influence which is hard to assess, but which was certainly significant.

By no means all the features of Russian society rejected by Tolstoy can be accepted as unmitigated evils. Among them was, after all, Russian literature itself – and indeed the world's art as a whole. Much of this – including the works of Shakespeare, Homer and Wagner, as well as his own early writings – was denounced by Tolstoy in critical studies which include *What is Art?* (1897).

The world in general has not accepted Tolstoy's verdict on aesthetic matters – or on anything else either – and though imperial Russia may sometimes seem unattractive in its political and social aspects, Russian nineteenth-century literature – not least that written by Tolstoy himself – remains unchallenged as the Empire's most abiding achievement.

Select bibliography

Sections 1 to 3 contain works written in or available in English, which may be found suitable for further reading. Section 4 is simply a list of other works, whether in English or not, to which reference happens to be made in the text or which have been found particularly useful. Though this section contains much interesting material, it is not intended as a systematic list for recommended reading, many of the works concerned being specialised or not easily accessible. Nor is this section offered as a comprehensive indication of source material.

An asterisk is occasionally used when more than one edition of a work is mentioned to indicate the edition to which reference has been made in the text.

1 WORKS ON NINETEENTH-CENTURY LITERATURE

Bayley, John, *Tolstoy and the Novel* (London, 1966)
— *Pushkin: a Comparative Commentary* (Cambridge, 1971)
Berlin, Isaiah, *The Hedgehog and the Fox: An Essay on Tolstoy's View of History* (London, 1953)
— *Fathers and Children: the Romanes Lecture* (Oxford, 1972)
Borras, F.M., *Maxim Gorky the Writer: an Interpretation* (Oxford, 1967)
Christian, R.F., *Tolstoy's 'War and Peace': a Study* (Oxford, 1962)
— *Tolstoy: a Critical Introduction* (Cambridge, 1969)
Fennell, John, ed., *Studies of Ten Russian Writers* (London, 1973)
Frank, Joseph, *Dostoevsky: the Seeds of Revolt, 1821–1849* (Princeton, 1976)
Freeborn, Richard, *Turgenev: the Novelist's Novelist* (Oxford, 1960)
— *The Rise of the Russian Novel: Studies in the Russian Novel from 'Eugene Onegin' to 'War and Peace'* (Cambridge, 1973)
Harkins, William E., *Dictionary of Russian Literature* (New York, 1956)
Hingley, Ronald, *Chekhov: a Biographical and Critical Study* (London, 1950)
— *The Undiscovered Dostoyevsky* (London, 1962)
— *A New Life of Anton Chekhov* (London, 1976)

Jones, Malcolm V., *Dostoyevsky: the Novel of Discord* (London, 1976)
Lavrin, Janko, *Goncharov* (Cambridge, 1954)
— *Lermontov* (Cambridge, 1959)
Magarshack, David, *Chekhov: a Life* (London, 1952)
— *Turgenev: a Life* (London, 1954)
— *Gogol: a Life* (London, 1957)
— *Dostoevsky* (London, 1962)
Matthewson, Rufus W., *The Positive Hero in Russian Literature*, 2nd edition (Stanford, 1975)
Maude, Aylmer, *The Life of Tolstoy: First Fifty Years* and *Later Years*, 2 vols (London, 1930)
Mirsky, D.S., *A History of Russian Literature*, ed. and abridged by Francis J. Whitfield (London, 1949*): a combined and abridged version of Mirsky's *Contemporary Russian Literature, 1881–1925* (London, 1926) and *History of Russian Literature from Earliest Times to the Death of Dostoevsky, 1881* (London, 1927)
Mochulsky, Konstantin, *Dostoyevsky: his Life and Work*. Tr. from the Russian with an Introduction by Michael A. Minihan (Princeton, 1967)
Moser, Charles A., *Antinihilism in the Russian Novel of the 1860s* (The Hague, 1964)
Peace, Richard, *Dostoyevsky: an Examination of the Major Novels* (Cambridge, 1971)
Simmons, Ernest J., *Pushkin* (Cambridge, Mass., 1937)
— *Leo Tolstoy* (Boston, 1946)
— *Dostoyevsky: the Making of a Novelist* (New York, 1950)
— *Chekhov: a Biography* (Boston, 1962)
— *Introduction to Tolstoy's Writings* (Chicago, 1968)
Slonim, Marc, *The Epic of Russian Literature: from its Origins through Tolstoy* (New York, 1950)
— *Modern Russian Literature: from Chekhov to the Present* (New York, 1953)
Troyat, Henri, *Tolstoy* (London, 1968)
— *Pushkin* (London, 1974)
— *Gogol: the Biography of a Divided Soul* (London, 1974) (all tr. from the French by Nancy Amphoux)
Yarmolinsky, Avrahm, *Dostoevsky: his Life and Art* (New York, 1957)
— *Turgenev: the Man, his Art and his Age* (New York, 1959)

2 GENERAL HISTORIES AND SURVEYS OF RUSSIA

Auty, R. and Obolensky, D., *Companion to Russian Studies: an Introduction to Russian History* (Cambridge)

Billington, James H., *The Icon and the Axe: an Interpretative History of Russian Culture* (London, 1966)
Charques, Richard, *A Short History of Russia* (London, 1956)
Chew, Allen F., *An Atlas of Russian History: Eleven Centuries of Changing Borders* (London, 1967)
Custine, A. de, *Russia*, abridged from the French (London, 1855)
Florinsky, Michael T., *Russia: a History and an Interpretation*, 2 vols (New York, 1953)
Freeborn, Richard, *A Short History of Modern Russia* (London, 1966)
Gilbert, Martin, *Russian History Atlas* (London, 1972)
Hingley, Ronald, *A Concise History of Russia* (London, 1972)
Hoetzsch, Otto, *The Evolution of Russia*, tr. from the German by Rhys Evans (London, 1966)
Karpovich, Michael, *Imperial Russia, 1801–1917* (New York, 1932)
Kochan, Lionel, *The Making of Modern Russia* (London, 1962)
Kornilov, A.A., *Modern Russian History*, tr. from the Russian by A.S. Kaun (New York, 1943)
Leroy-Beaulieu, A., *The Empire of the Tsars and the Russians*, tr. from the French by Z. Ragozine (New York, 1893–6)
Mackenzie Wallace, D., *Russia*, 2 vols (London, 1877*); also later edition (London, 1912)
Pares, B., *A History of Russia*, 2nd edition (New York, 1928)
Pipes, Richard, *Russia under the Old Regime* (London, 1974)
Platonov, S.F., *History of Russia*, tr. from the Russian by D. Aronsberg (New York, 1925)
Riasanovsky, Nicholas V., *A History of Russia* (New York, 1963)
Seton-Watson, Hugh, *The Russian Empire, 1801–1917* (Oxford, 1967)
Sumner, B.H., *Survey of Russian History* (London, 1944)
Szamuely, Tibor, *The Russian Tradition* (London, 1974)
Utechin, S.V., *Everyman's Concise Encyclopaedia of Russia* (London, 1961)

3 STUDIES OF ASPECTS OF THE RUSSIAN EMPIRE

Allen, W.E.D., *History of the Georgian People* (London, 1932)
— *The Ukraine: a History* (Cambridge, 1950)
Billington, James H., *Mikhailovsky and Russian Populism* (Oxford, 1958)
Blum, Jerome, *Lord and Peasant in Russia from the Ninth to the Nineteenth Century* (Princeton, 1961; New York, 1964*)
Bruford, W.H., *Chekhov and his Russia: a Sociological Study* (London, 1948)
Carr, Edward Hallett, *The Romantic Exiles: a Nineteenth Century Portrait Gallery* (London, 1933)
— *Michael Bakunin* (London, 1937)

Conybeare, Frederick C., *Russian Dissenters* (Cambridge, Mass., 1921)

Curtiss, John Sheldon, *Church and State in Russia: the Last Years of the Empire, 1900–1917* (New York, 1940)

Emmons, Terence, *The Russian Landed Gentry and the Peasant Emancipation of 1861* (Cambridge, 1968)

Footman, David, *Red Prelude: a Life of A.I. Zhelyabov* (London, 1944)

Greenberg, Louis, *The Jews in Russia*, 2 vols (New Haven, 1944–51)

Hare, Richard, *Pioneers of Russian Social Thought* (London, 1951)

Herzen, Alexander, *My Past and Thoughts*, tr. from the Russian by Constance Garnett, 6 vols (London, 1924–7)

Hingley, Ronald, *Nihilists* (London, 1967)

— *The Tsars: Russian Autocrats, 1533–1917* (London, 1968)

— *Russian Revolution* (London, 1970)

— *The Russian Secret Police: Muscovite, Imperial Russian and Soviet Political Security Operations, 1565–1970* (London, 1970)

Keep, J.L.H., *The Rise of Social Democracy in Russia* (Oxford, 1963)

Kennan, George, *Siberia and the Exile System*, 2 vols (New York, 1891)

Kennan, George F., *The Marquis de Custine and his Russia in 1839* (London, 1972)

Kochan, Lionel, *The Jews in Soviet Russia since 1917* (London, 1970)

Kolarz, Walter, *Religion in the Soviet Union* (London, 1961)

Lampert, E., *Studies in Rebellion* (London, 1957)

— *Sons against Fathers: Studies in Russian Radicalism and Revolution* (Oxford, 1965)

Longworth, Philip, *The Cossacks* (London, 1969)

Malia, Martin E., *Alexander Herzen and the Birth of Russian Socialism* (Cambridge, Mass., 1961)

Masaryk, T.G., *The Spirit of Russia*, tr. E. and C. Paul, with additional chapters by J. Slavik, 2 vols (London, 1955)

Mavor, James, *An Economic History of Russia*, 2nd edition, 2 vols (London, 1925)

Mazour, Anatole G., *The First Russian Revolution, 1825: The Decembrist Movement* (Stanford, 1937)

Miliukov, Paul, *Outlines of Russian Culture*, ed. Michael Karpovich, Part I: *Religion and the Church;* Part II: *Literature;* Part III: *Architecture, Painting and Music* (Philadelphia, 1942)

Monas, Sidney, *The Third Section: Police and Society in Russia under Nicholas I* (Cambridge, Mass., 1961)

Mosse, W.E., *Alexander II and the Modernization of Russia* (London, 1958)

Nikitenko, Aleksandr, *The Diary of a Russian Censor*, abridged, edited and translated from the Russian by Helen Saltz Jacobson (Amherst, Mass., 1975)

Raeff, Marc, *Russian Intellectual History: an Anthology* (New York, 1966)

Riasanovsky, Nicholas V., *Nicholas I and Official Nationality in Russia, 1825–1855* (Berkeley, 1959)

Robinson, Geroid T., *Rural Russia under the Old Régime*, 2nd printing (New York, 1949)

Semyonov, Yuri, *Siberia: its Conquest and Development*, tr. from the German by J.R. Foster (London, 1963)

Squire, P.S., *The Third Department: the Establishment and Practices of the Political Police in the Russia of Nicholas I* (Cambridge, 1968)

Stepniak (S.M. Kravchinsky), *Underground Russia*, 2nd edition (London, 1883)

— *The Russian Peasantry: their Agrarian Condition, Social Life and Religion*, new edition (New York, 1905)

Troyat, Henri, *Daily Life in Russia under the Last Tsar*, tr. from the French by Malcolm Barnes (London, 1961)

Tupper, Harmon, *To the Great Ocean: Siberia and the Trans-Siberian Railway* (London, 1965)

Utechin, S.V., *Russian Political Thought: a Concise History* (New York, 1964)

Venturi, Franco, *Roots of Revolution*, tr. from the Italian by Francis Haskell (London, 1959)

Westwood, J.N., *A History of Russian Railways* (London, 1964)

Wittram, Reinhard, *Russia and Europe*, tr. from the German by Patrick and Hanneluise Doran (London, 1973)

Yarmolinsky, Avrahm, *Road to Revolution: a Century of Russian Radicalism* (London, 1957)

4 OTHER WORKS

Aleksandrov, V.A. and others, ed., *Narody yevropeyskoy chasti SSSR* [The peoples of the European part of the U.S.S.R.] (Moscow, 1964)

Baedeker, Karl, *Russland, nebst Teheran, Port Arthur, Peking* [Russia with Port Arthur, Teheran and Pekin], 7th edition (Leipzig, 1912)

Burnaby, Fred., *A Ride to Khiva: Travels and Adventures in Central Asia* (London, 1876)

Edwards, Sutherland, *Russians at Home: Unpolitical Sketches* (London, 1861)

Gernet, M.N., *Istoriya tsarskoy tyurmy* [History of the Tsarist prison], 2nd edition, 3 vols (Moscow, 1951*), also 3rd edition, 5 vols (Moscow, 1960–4)

Hingley, Ronald, ed., *The Oxford Chekhov*, vol. iii (London, 1964); vol. viii (London, 1965)

Isayev, Andrey, '*Velikorusskiye plemena Moskovskoy oblasti*' [The Great

Russians of the Moscow Region] in: *Zhivopisnaya Rossiya* [Picturesque Russia], ed. P.P. Semyonov, vol. vi, part ii (St Petersburg, 1898)

Kjellberg, Lennart, *Den klassiska romanens Ryssland* [Russia of the classical novel] (Stockholm, 1964)

Kovalevsky, V.I., ed., *Rossiya v kontse XIX veka* [Russia at the end of the nineteenth century] (St Petersburg, 1900*); tr. into French as *La Russie à la fin du XIX siècle* (Paris, 1900)

Pushkin, A.S., *Eugene Onegin: a Novel in Verse*, ed., tr. and commentary by V. Nabokov, 4 vols (New York, 1964)

Rozenberg, Vl. and Yakushkin, V., *Russkaya pechat i tsenzura v proshlom i nastoyashchem* [The Russian press and censorship, past and present] (Moscow, 1905)

Schlesinger, M.L., *Land und Leute in Russland* [Land and people in Russia], 2nd edition (Berlin, 1909)

Turgenev, I.S., *Sobraniye sochineniy* [Collected works], 12 vols (Moscow, 1954)

Vinogradov, V.V., and others, ed., *Chekhov: Literaturnoye nasledstvo* [Literary heritage: Chekhov] (Moscow, 1960)

Woolf, Virginia, 'The Russian point of View'; in *The Common Reader*, First Series (London, 1938)

Index